Language Distribution Issues in Bilingual Schooling

Multilingual Matters

Please contact us for the latest book information:
Multilingual Matters, Bank House, 8a Hill Road,
Clevedon, Avon BS21 7HH, England.

MULTILINGUAL MATTERS 56
Series Editor: Derrick Sharp

Language Distribution Issues in Bilingual Schooling

Edited by

Rodolfo Jacobson and Christian Faltis

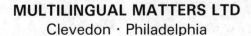
MULTILINGUAL MATTERS LTD
Clevedon · Philadelphia

Library of Congress Cataloging-in-Publication Data

Language distribution issues in bilingual schooling / edited by
 Rodolfo Jacobson and Christian Faltis.
  p. cm. (Multilingual matters ; 56)
  Includes index.
  1. Education, Bilingual. 2. Native language and education.
I. Jacobson, Rodolfo. II. Faltis, Christian, 1950–
III. Series: Multilingual matters (Series) ; 56.
LC3715.L36   1989   88-27019
371.97—dc19   CIP

British Library Cataloguing in Publication Data

Language distribution issues in bilingual
  schooling
  1. Bilingual education
  I. Jacobson, Rodolfo, *1915–*
  II. Faltis, Christian, *1951–*
  371.97

  ISBN 1-85359-046-0
  ISBN 1-85359-045-2 Pbk

Multilingual Matters Ltd
Bank House, 8a Hill Road   &   1900 Frost Road, Suite 101
Clevedon, Avon BS21 7HH   Bristol, PA 19007
England   U.S.A.

Copyright © 1990 Rodolfo Jacobson, Christian Faltis
and the authors of individual chapters.

Index compiled by Meg Davies (Society of Indexers).
Typeset by MCS, Salisbury.
Printed and bound in Great Britain by WBC Print, Bristol

Contents

SECTION IV: SPECIAL CASES

Introduction

RODOLFO JACOBSON and CHRISTIAN FALTIS

Bilingual schooling implies, by definition, the presence of two languages in the instructional process. Surprisingly, however, very little research and writing has been done on the issue of how the two languages are and should be distributed for content instruction in bilingual classrooms. Hence, the editors of this volume feel that it is timely to gather together the thoughts of language specialists, researchers and educators in order to explore how two languages may be effectively distributed in classrooms where more than one language is used to teach the content areas. The resulting volume consists of four major sections. Section I: *Language Distribution Issues and Ideas* introduces the complexities of language distribution issues. Topics related to classroom interaction is the focus of Section II: *Interactional Considerations*. Section III: *Technological Advances* examines the relationship of dual language use to computers and other instructional innovations found in bilingual classrooms. Finally, Section IV: *Special Cases* presents some special applications in the areas of Quechua–Spanish and French–English code-switching. The first section of the book consists of four chapters, while the remaining three sections contain two chapters each.

In Chapter 1 of the volume, Rodolfo Jacobson proposes a basic typology of bilingual methodology in his study on 'Allocating Two Languages as a Key Feature of a Bilingual Methodology'. The categories and subcategories suggested allow Jacobson to identify ten different options from which bilingual or ESL teachers can select when teaching students whose first language differs from that of the school. He argues that specifications of this nature are necessary to achieve a clear conception of what a teacher can do in classrooms where students speaking a minority language are engaged in learning school subjects taught in the majority language. Going beyond the theoretical discussion of bilingual typology, Jacobson provides examples of Spanish–English discourse to show how the same lesson content might be taught following each of the ten approaches. While practical applications of the theoretical models are often excluded from scholarly discussions, one of the expressed purposes of this chapter is to combine theory with practice in ways that help readers see the connection between the two.

Educators like Jacobson who have proposed specific bilingual teaching models often seek to implement the approaches they have designed. More commonly, however, educators conduct research in selected schools in order to describe and evaluate the effectiveness of existing models of teaching. Judith Walker de Felix's chapter on 'Language Use and New Trends in Research on Effective Bilingual/ESL Classrooms' exemplifies the second area of interest. Walker de Felix recognizes the importance of the conceptual framework for assessment purposes and argues that pundits of bilingual programs ought to be addressing *how* and not *whether* bilingual education is effective. Recent studies by Tikunoff and Wong Fillmore provide some relevance to the effectiveness question by focusing on effective teaching behaviors in classrooms serving language minority children. However, the general lack of professional litera-ture on the topic of effective programs, Walker de Felix comments, provides opponents of bilingual education lots of room to criticize it. With regard to English as a Second Language programs, she sees an even greater shortage of literature on effective teaching. Arguing that an adequate evaluation of classroom interaction in bilingual as well as ESL programs is needed, Walker de Felix stresses the importance of taking into consideration not only how language is used during interaction, but also how the teacher uses time to engage students in meaningful tasks. Like Jacobson, Walker de Felix advo-cates that more research be undertaken to 'test the effects of extant models of language use' as well as to build on current sociolinguistic frameworks in an effort to arrive at a more solid theoretical structure for future investigations.

In the following chapter, Robert Milk examines the issues of language attitudes, language use patterns, and the goals of the school in order to stress the all-encompassing role of language distribution in the bilingual classroom. Entitled 'Integrating Language and Content: Implications for Language Distribution in Bilingual Classrooms', Milk's study shares with the previous author a concern for two major issues: (1) how learning can best be achieved in a bilingual environment, and (2) the nature of effective classroom interaction, but goes beyond these by focusing on the changing nature of ESL methodology from grammar-based instruction to content-based integration. He also refers to Tikunoff with special emphasis on 'the integration of English language development with regular in-class instruction' and argues strongly in favor of the use of the second language 'as a medium of instruction as one of the best ways to develop and extend a learner's proficiency in that language'.

Milk suggests that an early concern for time spent in the target language has led to a simplistic view that quantitative matters were more important than qualitative ones when two languages are used for instruction. Milk characterizes ideal language learning contexts as those which involve the negotiation of meaning. He sees the need for greater integration of language and content in bilingual programs. Milk concludes his study by referring to one of the features advanced by proponents of sheltered-English programs, that of the careful separation of languages of instruction, and warns that prohibition of access to the native language becomes a highly debatable proposition when the primary goal of instruction is academic content. (For a viewpoint against the necessary separation of languages for content instruction, also see the first chapter of this volume. The Editors.)

The significance of ESL in content instruction and as a rationale for improving L2 acquisition for speakers of minority language was the focus of the previous two chapters. Christian Faltis takes the reader back in full circle to the concurrent use of English and the learner's home language, but with a special emphasis on teacher performance and on the evaluation of the performance. In his chapter entitled 'New Directions in Bilingual Research Design: The Study of Interactive Decision Making', Faltis starts out by focusing on the instructional variables of language sequencing and time distribution and their importance for mainstream language learning. He then analyzes the reasons why, even though the balanced use of the two languages has been recognized by most researchers as both desirable and appropriate, bilingual teachers tend to use English more than the students' native language for content instruction. He points out that the strict separation of two languages required by most bilingual programs is not faithfully adhered to and that in such programs the pull exerted by the power of English leads teachers to use it a majority of time. In contrast to the strict separation approach, it is possible for 'both languages to be used during content instruction, but with clearly expressed guidelines for how switching from one language to another is to occur'. It is at this point that Faltis describes the New Concurrent Approach proposed by Jacobson in Chapter 1, paying particular attention to the criteria that govern the NCA. The decision of bilingual teachers to use two languages in the classroom is then related to decision making in terms of 'when and why to use a given language for interaction with students during classroom instruction'. Faltis discusses existing decision making models and proposes his own conceptualization of one of the models presented, but incorporates multiple antecedents to interactive decision making using Jacobson's cue system. The proposed model is illustrated in a flow chart with the intent of offering 'an analytical framework in order to begin studying how bilingual teachers who use two languages during content instruction make decisions about when to use which language and what triggers that decision'. In the final section of the paper, Faltis refers to the *Stimulated Recall Technique* that lends itself quite naturally to the assessment of how teachers make interaction decisions as they implement the cited dual language approach.

Section II, with its emphasis on *Interactional Considerations* leads the reader from methodological concerns to the actual assessment of language performance in bilingual classrooms. The first chapter of this section was written by J. David Ramirez and Barbara Merino and it is entitled 'Classroom Talk in English Immersion, Early-Exit and Late-Exit Transitional Bilingual Education Programs'. The authors report on observations conducted throughout the United States in 103 first and second grade bilingual and immersion classrooms. Working from the premise that little is known about how instructional programs designed for limited English proficient (LEP) students actually function within the classroom, the authors sought out the answers to two important questions: (1) How is language used in the classroom for instruction? and (2) What are effective teaching behaviors in second language programs? The study begins with some background information on bilingual programs and ways to study them. Four alternative instructional programs are introduced and special emphasis is given to how, in principle, the programs are intended to differ from one another. The authors also consider the various ways researchers have investigated language use patterns and effective teaching behaviors and give examples of process, process/context, process/product, and process/process research designs.

After thoroughly describing their own research design and procedures, Ramirez and Merino present the results of their investigation in terms of questions and answers which inform the reader on issues such as (a) classroom language use, (b) what teachers talk about, (c) what types of questions teachers ask, (d) the extent to which teachers use realia, (e) what students say, and (f) how often students initiate conversations with their teachers. In summing up their findings, Ramirez and Marino focus on program differences and similarities as these relate to classroom language use, and then suggest several variables that can lead to high student interaction input. Their findings appear to confirm current research findings concerning the correlation between teachers' abilities to separate the two languages over longer periods of time and successful teaching performance, although the patterns of separation were different across the programs they examined. (For a different view, see Chapters 1 and 4 of Section I in this volume. The Editors.) Finally, Ramirez and Merino bring out the point that teachers tended to dominate classroom talk in all of the programs they observed, while at the same time, students contributed relatively little to classroom discussions.

In the following chapter entitled 'Instructional Discourse in "Effective" Hispanic Classrooms', Eugene Garcia takes a different approach to classroom interaction research in that he focuses exclusively on successful classroom performances as a means to explore what makes the discourse occurring in these classrooms work so well. Garcia stresses the point that a 'primary issue in instruction of Hispanic children is *understanding instructional interaction*' (emphasis ours). To introduce the reader to the issue from a Hispanic perspective, Garcia reviews a number of studies concerned with understanding language choice patterns of young bilinguals. He argues that in order to understand early childhood bilingualism, researchers need to consider the child's surrounding environment, especially how it provides a model to the child for learning ways of interaction. The research Garcia presents in this chapter purposefully draws on as well as builds upon previous research on bilingual interaction, but has a special emphasis on teacher–student and student–student interactions in highly selective classrooms. Garcia bases his analysis of interaction on the notion that 'teaching is a fundamental act of two-way interaction between teacher and students'. His model of analysis concentrates on the sequential characteristics of teacher–student interactions inspired by Hugh Mehan's model of instructional interaction sequences. Garcia, however, introduces some modifications to the Mehan model in order to accommodate his data. This allows him to assess the 'instructional style of "effective" teachers of Hispanic students', the primary purpose of the study.

Garcia reports the results of his study by focusing on instructional discourse and language use. His findings confirm certain characteristics of teaching styles previously reported by others, but also identify additional ones that have not been discussed elsewhere. His most significant finding involves student-to-student interaction discourse strategies corresponding to social motives prevalent in some Mexican American families. Specifically, Garcia found that students in effective classrooms make creative use of the language as they interact among themselves after the teacher has provided instructional initiation. This finding contradicts the results in the previous chapter that teachers do most of the talking and that students contribute little to classroom discussion. Thus, it appears that classrooms must be especially effective to reveal the kinds of creativity bilingual students can display with appropriate guidance from the teacher.

Section III examines *Technological Advances* in the use of interactive video systems, computers, and cooperative learning for teaching bilingual students. In his chapter entitled 'Bilingual Interactive Video: Let the Student Switch Languages', Raymond Padilla reports on the potential use of interactive video systems (IVS) for bilingual instruction. Padilla begins the chapter by pointing out that IVS offer an additional way to implement concurrent (non-translation) language use as an instructional strategy. (The other justifiable way being the NCA discussed in Chapters 1 and 4. The Editors.) An important feature of IVS is that it puts the student in control of the language of instruction, meaning that the user controls both the language of input and the language of response. The IVS used in the present study was designed to allow students to select monolingual instruction in L1 or L2 or bilingual instruction. The only switching constraint for the bilingual instruction option was that students were allowed to switch between languages only at the end of each unit or between lessons, both of which were relatively short in duration.

Professor Padilla was interested in finding out how bilingual students responded to bilingual IVS as a result of learning how to operate a learning lesson using a system of interactive video disks tied into interactive personal computers. Moreover, because language switching was an important feature of the IVS, he was also interested in learning how bilingual students would use the two languages during the learning lessons.

The results of the study indicate that students respond favorably to virtually all aspects of bilingual interaction video instruction. Regarding language use, Padilla found that students selected about equally between L1 and L2 to initiate instruction. Relatively little language switching occurred between instruction units and lessons, even though such switching was easy to accomplish. That switching between languages did not occur is a finding 'that needs to be interpreted cautiously...', especially since the constraints placed upon switching were quite dissimilar to those found in more natural contexts where language switching is commonplace. Padilla ends the chapter with a discussion of important limitations of interaction video technology in general, and a call for new and more extensive research on bilingual interactive video technology.

In the following chapter, Robert DeVillar offers readers a provocative look at how computer assisted instruction combined with innovative instructional practices can facilitate talk in English between speakers with different levels of English language proficiency. DeVillar's chapter is entitled 'Second Language Use within the Non-Traditional Classroom: Computers, Cooperative Learning, and Bilingualism'. The chapter begins with a thorough discussion and comparison of opportunities for second language acquisition within the elementary school setting between (1) whole-class, teacher fronted instruction (a traditional practice) and (2) cooperative learning and computer assisted instruction (non-traditional practices). The discussion serves as an introduction to his study concerning language use within and between dyads of students who were engaged in an information gap task, computer assisted setting within a sixth grade classroom. Following a complete description of the methodology used, DeVillar presents the results of his study, in terms of (a) word production in the two languages, (b) the role of English and English language proficiency, (c) the effect of grouping by English language proficiency, (d) utterance complexity and grouping strategies, and (e) task assignments and language use.

The results of the study lead DeVillar to suggest two important implications for second language opportunities in a bilingual classroom. The first implication concerns grouping strategies that take English language proficiency into account. DeVillar found that substantial English language practice is possible with students who are at the same level of proficiency, limited through fluent, and with students who are at different levels of proficiency, as long as one of them was not extremely low English proficient. With extremely low English proficient students, only the native English speaker serving as a dyad partner will be able to generate enough talk to accomplish a two way language task. The second implication concerns grouping dyads in relation to the particular learning objective. DeVillar makes the very important point that the composition of groups for learning depends upon the intent of the learning objective. Thus, if the primary objective of a lesson were L2 development, then grouping lower English proficient students with native English speakers would be most effective. However, if the intent were to increase content knowledge, then the teacher could effectively group students in mixed non-native English proficiency dyads.

The final two chapters of the book are presented in Section IV, which deals with *Special Cases*. Both chapters address the use of two languages for instruction, but they do so in settings not normally discussed in the literature on bilingual education. The first special case involves a study by Nancy Hornberger entitled 'Teacher Quechua Use in Bilingual and Non-Bilingual Classrooms of Puno, Peru'. This chapter draws on data from a two-year ethnographic study carried out in several Quechua-speaking communities of Puno, Peru to describe teacher Quechua use during lesson time in both bilingual and non-bilingual classrooms. Hornberger presents descriptive data relating to the (1) amount of Quechua use, (2) types of teacher talk realized in Quechua, and (3) types of code-switching between Quechua and Spanish. Hornberger's study sets out to test Jacobson's proposition (this volume) that the allocation of two languages in a bilingual program is a key feature of that program's methodology. Specifically, Hornberger argues that the way Quechua is used in the bilingual classrooms 'not only differentiates them from the non-bilingual classrooms but also is an indicator of the type of bilingual education the PEEB [Experimental Bilingual Education Project of Puno] is implementing'.

Through examples of the code-switching and patterns of language use in the two school settings, Hornberger presents a convincing argument for the effectiveness of bilingual schooling, especially when the program incorporates language usage patterns that are familiar to the students. Her conclusions are straightforward: '...we cannot help but conclude that Quechua children will achieve higher levels of language proficiency in the L1, Quechua, in the bilingual classroom than they did in the non-bilingual classroom'.

In the final chapter of this section and of the book as well, Professors Gerald Giauque and Christopher Ely write about a special way of using code-switching methodology for teaching beginning level French to university students. The approach is based upon the idea that 'the teacher speaks the foreign language using many cognate words, and uses CS (i.e. code-switching into English) to communicate those words which are not cognates in the target language'. The goal is to help students understand a great deal of the target language at an early phase of their experience with it. Giauque and Ely point out that their approach to code-switching differs from the one proposed by Jacobson for bilingual content-area teaching in that switches are done intra-sententially as opposed to inter-sententially, where the speaker continues in one language for at least the duration of a sentence before switching to the other language. They describe the general procedure used in the early weeks of instruction and provide the reader with background support for the notions and strategies employed. Here the reader is able to learn how intra-sentential code-switching can be used not only to increase comprehension, but also to encourage L2 interaction in speaking and writing between the teacher and students.

The final section of the chapter presents the results of a study that was designed to determine how well the procedure works with beginning level students. The results indicate that students benefited from the experience, and in the process, learned much about code-switching as a social and pedagogical phenomenon.

The volume ends with a short biographical sketch of each of the contributors.

We feel a great sense of appreciation to all of the contributors for sharing their insights and ideas, and we realize that the volume would not have been possible without them. We wish to thank our reviewers, several of whom read two or more papers, for their help throughout the development of this volume: Cindy Alvarez, Ernesto Bernal, George Blanco, Mauricio Charpenel, Barbara Flores, Gustavo Gonzalez, Roseann Gonzalez, Stephen Lafer, Mary McGroarty, Frances Morales, Nelson Rojas, Mindy Sperling, and Rosie Tinajero.

It is our hope that this collection of original papers will serve to stimulate additional research on issues concerned with the distribution of languages in bilingual settings.

Section I
Language Distribution Issues and Ideas

1 Allocating two languages as a key feature of a bilingual methodology

RODOLFO JACOBSON

Introduction

Bilingual methodology as a technical construct concerning how to teach children whose first language is not English has been grossly misunderstood by approaching it from the vantage points of either ethnic culture or lexical competency in the non-English language. Even though the knowledge of and the familiarity with both are important components of bilingual teacher training, they do not represent *per se* the core of bilingual methodology. As a matter of fact, a multicultural approach should underlie any viable educational method in the United States and the mastery of specialized terms needed for the teaching of mathematics or science or social studies is obviously a prerequisite of any sound instructional approach regardless of the language or languages of instruction. If the bilingual method is not justifiable on cultural nor lexical grounds, then on what grounds is it justifiable?

The author's recent research has gathered convincing evidence that it is the distributional pattern chosen for a given bilingual program that determines the method. In other words, the manner how the two languages are being allocated is ultimately indicative of the bilingual method being used. To elaborate on the above, the author proposes to describe the range of language distributional options available to the bilingual teacher and to briefly comment on his recent research findings that demonstrated the viability of some of these options.

1. Broad categories of language distribution and their rationales

It is obvious that two languages must be used as media of instruction if a bilingual focus is to be maintained in an educational program. Bilingual educators have usually insisted on the separation of the two languages, one of which is English and the other, the child's vernacular. By strictly separating the languages, the teacher avoids, it is argued, cross-contamination, thus making it easier for the child to acquire a new linguistic system as he/she internalizes a given lesson. This viewpoint was felt to be so self-evident that no research was ever conducted to support this argument. At the bottom of all this lies a rather poor conception of what a young mind is capable of, i.e. the child's incapability of sorting out language data belonging to two different sources and assigning them to two systems. Children in multilingual settings have shown to possess unusual talents that allow them to become, not only bilinguals, but polyglots regardless of how they have been exposed to the various linguistic sources. To be sure, language separation is one way of approaching the child's learning through two languages allowing him/her to become bilingual by means of two monolingual processes in which he/she associates one language with some experiences and the other language with others.

The insistence on language separation for bilingual programs has generated, by the very nature of this dogma, the opposition to the concurrent use of two languages. Again, it was felt that the inappropriateness of the concurrent use was so self-evident that no research had to be conducted to prove this fact. As language separation would lead to the uncontaminated acquisition of either language, the concurrent use of both languages would lead to confusion, mixing and highly accented speech patterns in the target language. Whether this latter argument could actually be upheld, should have been supported by hard data but, unfortunately, no research project in the past has ever explored this issue. More recently, however, data seem to suggest that certain forms of concurrent use can be as successful as are certain forms of language separation.

The notion of bilingual instruction can be expanded to mean instruction of bilingual children where 'bilingual' is interpreted as home-language-dominant and limited-English-proficient. Teaching such children in their weaker language (English) has recently been viewed as a means of upgrading their skills in the target language. Research in a different setting (Canada) has lately become available and educators in the United States are using in some programs the target language with children of other-language backgrounds without seriously analyzing these experiments in terms of (1) the similarities and differences between the two settings and (2) the degree of transferability of the Canadian design. Regardless of these concerns, it appears that some bilingual educators have become fascinated with the fact that *some* children can learn a second language well when they are exposed to it most or even all of the time, in particular when school subjects are being taught through that medium.

Three broad language distribution categories and their rationales have here been discussed. However, it has been noted that serious research evaluating the merits of each distributional category is still scarce. As a first step toward a clearer understanding of language distribution, one may wish to examine which subcategories of distributional patterns may lend themselves to begin gathering the methodological data that are so urgently needed.

2. Sub-categories of language distributional patterns

The two languages of a bilingual program can be separated on the basis of four criteria, i.e. *topic*, *person*, *time* and *place*. By topic we mean content or school subjects, such as deciding which language should become the medium of instruction for, say, one-half of the academic subjects and which language, for the other half. Such a decision could be content-free or content-sensitive. The former would involve a random split between school subjects in order to assign one language as a medium of instruction to one set and the other to the remaining set. The latter would involve the assignment of one language to those subjects that seem to be more appropriately taught in that language and that of the other language to the remainder of subjects for the very same reason. The content-sensitive topic-oriented language separation approach presents the difficulty of having to support the notion that one linguistic system is good, say, to teach social studies but not math or science and the other system, to teach math or science but not social studies. Whichever approach is followed it will lead to a design where the languages are separated by topic.

The separation of the two languages by person, in turn, requires the presence in the classroom of two persons, one of whom communicates consistently in English and the other, in the child's vernacular. Two teachers using a team approach, a teacher and an aide, a teacher and an interchangeable set of volunteer parents could all implement such a design. Children would soon become conditioned to the fact that a given language is chosen according to the person whom they address. The staff's normative behavior would eliminate for the child the need of assessing a particular communicative event first before engaging in a language choice event.

The time factor is probably easiest to control by posting a classroom schedule that calls for the use of English, say, in the mornings and that of the child's home language after lunch. Other time distribution on a regular or sporadic basis can be agreed on by posting signs at the door indicating which language would be used on a given day. The Alternate Day Approach used in the Philippines and described in the professional literature (G.R. Tucker, 1970: 281–300) is an example of the latter language separation approach on the basis of time.

The physical location (Cohen, 1975: 104–06) where a class is taught may serve as another consistent cue for the child to know whether English is the medium of communication or whether the home language, say, Spanish is expected. Where different rooms for these language-controlled activities are unavailable, activity centers can serve the same purpose of serving as an easy cue for the child to respond to.

The artificiality of language separation based on any of these criteria is obvious as in a real life situation neither topic nor person nor time nor place are easily controlled. Furthermore, the separation that can so be controlled, is uncontrollable within the mind. The child has only one mind where to internalize whichever information he/she has been exposed to. Unless such a mind is properly disciplined, there will always remain the risk of confusion or cross-contamination.

The two languages can also be used concurrently to ensure that the teacher's information is fully comprehended regardless of any lacunae in the target language that may still exist. How this is done may be crucial for both types of learning, the acquisition of language and that of factual knowledge. Again, four ways of language distribution in the learning of content can be identified. The teacher may randomly switch from one language to the other disregarding any principle of unilingual consistency within a sentence or between several sentences of the same thought group. Such a code-switching behavior is frequently observed in some situations in informal dialogs among bilingual ethnics and its use in school settings—controversial as it may appear—would simplify the decoding process for those children who have been exposed to this kind of verbal behavior. However, if the development of language is to go hand in hand with the acquisition of factual knowledge, caution with such a flipflopping procedure may be in order. On the other hand, the teacher may consistently alternate between the two languages by saying everything twice, in English and in the child's vernacular, in a way that reminds us of the consecutive interpretation used during court cases when defendants do not speak the language of the court. It has been argued that the translation into the child's vernacular of everything that is being taught may prevent him/her from ever developing the kind of English language proficiency that must be one of the objectives of a sound bilingual program. Unfortunately, no research data are available to support the fears concerning the use of flipflopping or concurrent translation in the classroom.

Thirdly, one may preview a school unit in the child's vernacular and teach it in depth in English. The reverse is equally possible: the unit is taught in English and then reviewed in the child's vernacular. The child who tries to gain his/her factual knowledge from the preview-review portions of the lesson may internalize a watered-down version of the topic, unless he/she makes a strong effort to use these portions only to fill in the gaps caused by his/her incomplete knowledge of English when the in-depth version of the lesson was presented.

An innovative model of teaching concurrently in the two languages has recently been proposed where a highly structured approach to code-switching is introduced. Here, the switching is only teacher-initiated, the alternation occurs mainly between thought groups and only when the teacher can justify it on several grounds and, finally, this dual language use is consciously incorporated in the lesson in response to certain cues that the teacher wishes to acknowledge. Some of the concerns that bilingual educators have upheld in regard to the concurrent use of two languages seem to be addressed here, i.e. there is no intra-sentential code-switching, the alternation is not random but purposeful, the use of both languages is fully balanced and the structure of the lesson does not encourage the child to tune out whilst his/her weaker language is spoken. Jacobson (1978, 1979a, 1979b, 1981a, 1981b, 1982, 1983a, 1983b, 1983c, 1985, 1988) who had been developing the *New Concurrent Approach* since 1975 tested it in a Federal project from 1981–84 (see below), thus being one of the very few who gathered hard data on specific methodological options in bilingual education.

The use of the target language—here, English—in teaching the child whose mother tongue differs from the school language can be carried out in two ways, similar in certain aspects but different in others. The similarity consists in the use of the target language as a medium of instruction. The difference, in turn, resides in such facts as (1) whether or not children are starting out alike with a zero level background in the target language, (2) whether or not they are members of the middle class with positive self-identity, (3) whether or not the teachers are balanced bilinguals who accept the children's language when necessary even though they may avoid its use in their own responses and (4) whether or not the further development of the mother tongue is of concern and provisions are made to that effect, in order not to alienate the children from their home environment

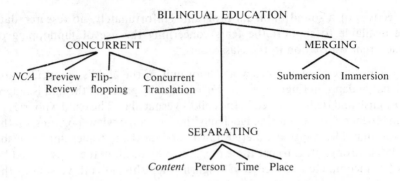

FIGURE 1 *Subcategories of language distributional patterns*

and their culture. The choice between immersion and submersion seems to be a subtle one based on the notions of additive as opposed to subtractive bilingualism and the role of the self-image in the language acquisitional process. On the other hand, both are language distributional practices that merit serious considerations when bilingual methodology is at issue.

Ten subcategories of language distributional patterns have been discussed on a somewhat theoretical plane. The figure above shows the relationship of these subcategories to the broader categories considered in Section 1, above.

It may now be pertinent to offer some actual examples of these subcategories, so that the nature of these options is understood more fully.

3. Bilingual methods illustrated

The difference between the various language distributional practices can best be appreciated if the content is kept stable and only the languages are selected variably to illustrate the methods discussed in the preceding section. The vernacular used in the example shall be Spanish and the objective of the lesson will be to review a science lesson concerning 'Air with regard to Weight and Space', and to recall an experiment demonstrating the fact that air has weight and takes up space. Depending on the method chosen, a portion of the cited lesson might be as follows:

LSA—Time

April 22—Today English is spoken
> T: Do you remember what we have been learning about air? What have we learned about air and weight?

S₁: ...that air has weight.

T: Very good; and what have we learned about air and space?

S₂: ...that air takes up space.

T: Excellent. And do you remember the experiment that we did the other day with the cup and the paper napkin?

S₃: We put a napkin on a cup with water and the paper did not get wet.

T: Very good. And who can tell me why the paper did not get wet when I turned the cup upside down?

S₄: ...because the air in the cup did not let the water through.

April 23—Hoy se habla español

T: Se recuerdan Uds., Clase, ¿qué aprendimos acerca del aire? ¿Qué aprendimos acerca del aire y del peso del aire?

S₁: ...que el aire pesa.

T: Muy bien y ¿qué aprendimos acerca del aire y del espacio que ocupa el aire?

S₂: ...que el aire ocupa espacio.

T: Excelente. Y ¿se recuerdan del experimento que hicimos el otro día con el vaso y la toallita de papel?

S₃: Pusimos una toallita encima de un vaso con agua y el papel no se mojó.

T: Muy bien. Y ¿quién me puede decir por qué no se mojó el papel cuando puse el vaso boca abajo?

S₄: ...porque el aire en el vaso no dejó pasar el agua.

LSA—Place

The English Room (or Activity Center)

T: We have learned that air has weight but what have we learned about air and space?

S₁: Air takes up space.

T: Good. And who remembers the experiment that we did the other day with the paper cup?

S₂: I do. We put a napkin on a cup with water.

T: Right. And what happened?

S₃: The paper did not get wet.

T: Why?

S₄: ...because the air did not let the water through.

El cuarto español (o el centro de actividades en español)

T: ¿Qué estudiamos hoy aquí?

S₁: Ciencias.

T: Entonces ¿estudiamos lo mismo que tuvimos en el otro cuarto?

S₂: No, allá fué 'science.'

T: Muy bien, Clase, aquí es ciencias porque hablamos en español. ¿Se recuerdan del experimento que hicimos entonces con un vaso de cartón y una toallita de papel?

S₃: Sí, pusimos una toallita en un vaso.

T: Y ¿qué más?

S₄: La toallita no se mojó cuando puso el vaso boca abajo.

LSA—Person

The Classroom Teacher (English)

T: Air has weight and it also takes up space. Did you know that, class?

S₁: Yes, Miss, like in the experiment.

T: Who else remembers that experiment?

S₂: I do. We put a napkin on a paper cup.

T: And...

S₃: The paper did not get wet.

T: Why?

S₄: ...because of the air in the cup.

T: Very good. Mrs. Gomez will now review that lesson a bit more.

La asistente de la maestra (Español)

A: ¿Qué me pueden decir del aire?

S₁: ...que el aire pesa.

A: Bien, y ¿qué más?

S₂: ...que ocupa espacio

A: Muy bien. Y ¿qué hizo Mrs. Jones con el vaso?

S₃: Lo puso boca abajo.

A: ¿Sí? Y ¿por qué?

S₄: Para ver si el agua mojaba el papel.

LSA—Topic

Science

T: Do you remember what we have been learning about air? What have we learned about air and weight?

S₁: ...that air has weight.

T: Very good; and what have we learned about air and space?

S₂: ...that air takes up space.

T: Excellent. And do you remember the experiment that we did the other day with the cup and the paper napkin?

S₃: We put a napkin on a cup with water and the paper did not get wet.

T: Very good. And who can tell me why the paper did not get wet when I turned the cup upside down?
S4: ...because the air in the cup did not let the water through.

Estudios sociales
T: ¿Quién sabe que es lo que hace el cartero?
S1: Es un señor que trae las cartas y los paquetes.
T: Muy bien y ¿tú has recibido una carta alguna vez?
S2: Sí, muchas veces.
T: Y ¿quiénes te escribieron?
S3: Mi papá y una vez, mi abuelo.
T: ¿De dónde te escribió tu abuelo?
S4: ...de México.

CA—Flipflopping
T: ¿Se recuerdan Uds. de lo que aprendimos about air? ¿Qué es lo que aprendimos about air and weight?
S1: ... que el aire pesa.
T: Muy bien. And what have we learned about air and space?
S2: ...que el aire ocupa espacio.
T: Excelente. Y ¿se recuerdan Uds. del experimento que hicimos el otro día? The one with the cup and the paper napkin.
S3: We put a napkin on a cup con agua y el papel no se mojó.
T: Y ¿quién me dice why the paper did not get wet?
S4: ...porque the air in the cup did not let the water through.

CA—Preview/Review
T: Hoy vamos a repasar la lección del aire que estudiamos ayer. Dijimos que el aire pesa y que ocupa espacio, ¿se recuerdan?
S1: Si, señora Jones, y también hicimos un experimento que me gustó mucho.
T: Muy bien. Entonces vamos a ver que es que recordamos. Air has weight. That is very important, class. And what did we say about space?
S2: Air takes up space.
T: Yes and we showed that in our experiment with the paper cup. What else did we use in the experiment?
S3: A kleenex.
T: Yes, we used a paper napkin.
S4: And water.

T: We put some water in the cup and then we covered it with a napkin. Did the water spill when we turned the cup?

S5: No, the air did not let it through.

CA—Translation

T: We learned yesterday that air has weight. Ayer dijimos que el aire pesa. And what have we learned about air and space? Y ¿qué aprendimos acerca del aire y el espacio?

S1: ...que el aire ocupa espacio.

T: You are right, air takes up space. And we also did an experiment. ¿No se recuerdan del experimento que hicimos?

S2: Si, con un vaso de cartón.

T: Did we use anything else besides the paper cup? ¿Qué más usamos?

S3: Una toallita de papel.

S4: Y le pusimos agua al vaso.

T: You are right, we put some water in the cup and then, we covered it all up with a napkin. And what did I do then? ¿Qué hice yo entonces?

S5: Ud. puso el vaso boca abajo.

T: Yes, I turned the cup upside down. And did the napkin get wet? ¿Se mojó la toallita de papel?

S6: No, se quedó sequita.

T: ¿Por qué? But why?

S7: Because of the air.

CA—NCA

T: Do you remember what we have been learning about air? What have we learned about air and weight?

S1: ...that air has weight.

T: Very good. And what have we learned about air and space?

S2: ...that air takes up space.

T: Very good. ¿Se recuerdan del experimento que hicimos el otro día con el vaso y la toallita de papel? ¿Me pueden decir lo que hicimos?

S3: Pusimos una toallita encima de un vaso y no se mojó el papel.

T: Muy bien. Who can tell me now why the paper didn't get wet?

S4: ...because the air in the cup didn't let the water into the napkin.

T: Muy bien. Tú sí pusiste atención. El papel no se mojó porque el aire ocupa espacio y no permite que entre el agua.

MA—Immersion

T: Do you remember what we have been learning about air?

S_1: Air? Oh, aire.

T: Yes, air and weight.

S_1: ...que el aire pesa.

T: Yes, air has weight.

S_1: Air has weight.

T: What about air and space?

S_2: Air ocupa espacio.

T: Yes, air takes up space. Who remembers the experiment that we did the other day?

S_3: With the cup and the napkin?

T: Yes, we covered a cup with a napkin. Was there some water in the cup?

S_4: Yes, water.

T: And what happened when I turned the cup over? Did the napkin get wet?

S_5: No, no se mojó.

T: It did not get wet because the air in the cup took up space.

MA—Submersion

T: Do you remember what we have been learning about air?

S_1: El aire pesa.

T: We don't want to speak Spanish, do we? Air has weight.

S_1: Air has weight.

T: What about space?

S_2: Espacio. Si, ocupa espacio.

T: Say: it takes up space.

S_2: It takes up space.

T: Good. We only want to speak English in class. Now tell me about the experiment.

S_3: With the cup and the napkin.

T: Did we put water into the cup?

S_4: Yes.

T: And did we cover it with the napkin?

S_5: No se mojó.

T: It did not get wet when I turned it over.

The discussion of the preceding sections makes it unnecessary to elaborate on these examples. They merely serve the purpose of illustrating the theoretical aspects alluded to above. A decision concerning which method works can not be made on speculative grounds. A series of research projects must be designed in order to gather data as to what works in bilingual education. Only the surface of such a research agenda has been scratched by conducting the Title VII Demonstration Project in Bilingual Instructional Methodology (1981-84) in San Antonio. The following section will briefly describe which methodological options have been explored in the cited project, what special issues have been addressed and which findings have emerged.

4. Title VII demonstration project in bilingual methodology

Two of the language distributional patterns described above were chosen as a basis for a Federal project in bilingual methodology. Its objective was to demonstrate the relative effectiveness of a language separation model (LSA—by school subjects) as compared to a concurrent model (NCA) by implementing over three years (1981–84) a carefully conceived design in two local schools. Indian Creek Elementary was selected as the site for the LSA Model and Sky Harbour Elementary for the NCA Model. Children of limited English language proficiency (LEP) were identified to participate in the Project with the understanding that they would not be exited prior to the completion of the Project in order to produce longitudinal data on bilingual methodology. Two Project classrooms operated in each school, hereby allowing the participating children to progress from grades K and 1 during the first year to grades 2 and 3 during the final year. The teaching staff consisted of four bilingual teachers and four bilingual aides so that each grade had the necessary personnel to implement the sophisticated design. A program coordinator and a project director were responsible, not only for its faithful implementation but also for the required staff development, in particular in the area of the less familiar NCA Model. The parent involvement component provided an opportunity to make the experiment relevant to the community as the social context for this program was deemed to be of crucial importance. Finally, a rigorous evaluation component served the purpose of monitoring the children's academic achievement and also of globally assessing the extent to which the Project achieved the overall objectives stated in the proposal.

In addition to the central objective of the Project, that of demonstrating the effectiveness of two bilingual approaches, several special issues emerged and were also addressed. A discussion of these issues is beyond the scope of the present study but the listing of the topics that were researched as the Project was progressing may be in order:

1. *The bilingual readiness program for level K* whose objective was to firmly establish Spanish as one of the language media to be used in the classroom;

2. The attention to *affective factors with emphasis on a classroom climate* favorable to bicultural–bilingual performances;
3. *The role of the first language* as medium through which cognitive skills can best be acquired;
4. *The communicative competence in bilingual settings* as a means of developing appropriate verbal interaction;
5. *The control of language choice* in order to promote the skills of language alternation as a function of person, place and topic; and
6. *The bilingual continuum* as a way of assessing children's degree of bilinguality in order to allow the teacher to strive for greater bilingual balance in their verbal behavior.

The findings of the Project have confirmed the viability of two bilingual methods, the LSA—topic and the NCA models. Both language goals were achieved as the children became proficient in English and developed their mother tongue to a degree that allowed them to learn through either language. The unproven hypothesis that children will mix the languages when taught in a language alternation mode was rejected, at least when the latter is, as in NCA, a carefully structured concurrent approach. All Project teachers predicted at the end of the last year that the participating children would not experience any learning problem in future years just because the medium of instruction would have shifted to English only. Having acquired in their home language the necessary cognitive skills to achieve academically and having transferred them to the school language as the latter became firmly established, the children began to display their academic potentials in various content areas. No significant difference emerged between groups regardless of whether the languages were separated or used concurrently. However, some trends emerged suggesting that mathematical skills were favored when languages were used concurrently but other skills were favored when languages were separated. The Project as a whole showed the effectiveness of a design that combines demonstration and research components as the results of several research tasks could be utilized and the effectiveness of the upgraded approach be demonstrated at once in a realistic setting. In this way, the earlier cited 'special issues' yielded valuable responses to crucial research questions and these responses, in turn, could then be incorporated into the normal routine of a bilingual classroom.

Conclusion

Of ten language distributional patterns only two (LSA by school subject and NCA) have been researched and been found to be viable methods for a bilingual program. The replication of the experiment is of course necessary to substantiate the claim that the two approaches are equally valid and should be implemented on a larger scale. The other eight bilingual options described above, in turn, have not yet been researched and attempts should be made to explore the degree of viability of each. Based upon the results of future research projects, teachers should be able to select the language distributional pattern that adjusts itself best to their personality and their teaching strategies and, by the same token, presents itself as the best possible means to reach limited English speaking children in order to bring about the academic achievement necessary for their success in an ever more demanding society.

References

COHEN, A. 1975, *A Sociolinguistic Approach to Bilingual Education*. Rowley, MA: Newbury House.

JACOBSON, R. 1978, Codeswitching in South Texas: Sociolinguistic consideration and pedagogical applications. *LASSO Journal* 3.1.

—— 1979a, Beyond ESL: The Teaching of Content Other than Language Arts in Bilingual Education. In R.' BAUMAN and J. SHERZER (eds), *Working Papers in Sociolinguistics*. Austin, TX: Southwest Educational Development Laboratory.

—— 1979b, Can bilingual teaching techniques reflect bilingual community behavior? A study in ethnoculture and its relationship to some amendments contained in the New Bilingual Education Act. In R. PADILLA (ed.), *Ethnoperspectives in Bilingual Education. Vol. 1: Bilingual Educational and Public Policy in the United States*. Ypsilanti, MI: Eastern Michigan University Press.

—— 1981a, Can and should the Laredo experiment be duplicated elsewhere? The applicability of the concurrent approach in other communities. In P.G. GONZALES (ed.), *Proceeding, Eighth Annual International Bilingual Bicultural Education Conference, Seattle, Washington*. Rosslyn, VA: National Clearinghouse for Bilingual Education.

—— 1981b, The implementation of a bilingual instruction model: The new concurrent approach. In R.V. PADILLA (ed.), *Ethnoperspectives in Bilingual Education Research. Vol. 3: Bilingual Education Technology*. Ypsilanti, MI: Eastern Michigan University Press.

—— 1982, The role of the vernacular in transitional bilingual education. In B. HARTFORD, A. VALDMAN and C.R. FOSTER (eds), *Issues in International Bilingual Education: The Role of the Vernacular*. New York: Plenum Press.

—— 1983a, Promoting concept and language development in the classroom. In S.S. SEIDNER (ed.), *Issues of Language Assessment* (II Language Assessment Institute Proceedings). Rosslyn, VA: National Clearinghouse for Bilingual Education.

—— 1983b, Intersentential Codeswitching: An Educationally Justifiable Strategy. ERIC ED 231 221.

—— 1983c, Can two languages be acquired concurrently? Recent developments in bilingual methodology. In H.B. ALTMAN and M. MCCLURE (eds), *Dimension: Language 1982*. Louisville, KY: University of Louisville Press.

—— 1985, Uncovering the covert bilingual: How to retrieve the hidden home language. In E. GARCIA and R. PADILLA (eds), *Advances in Bilingual Education Research*. Tucson, AZ: University of Arizona Press.

—— 1988, A new design for the qualitative assessment of children's language choice. *Sociolinguistics* 17.1.

TUCKER, G.R. 1970, An alternate day approach to bilingual education. In J.E. ALATIS (ed.), *Bilingualism and Language Contact* GURT, 1979. Washington, D.C.: Georgetown University Press.

2 Language use and new trends in research on effective bilingual/ESL classrooms

JUDITH WALKER DE FELIX

Issues in effective bilingual teaching literature

There is considerable evidence that bilingual education is an effective delivery system for developing English language skills (e.g. Hakuta, 1986; Troike, 1978; Willig, 1985). Public debate over how to best educate limited English proficient (LEP) children continues, however, in spite of this evidence. While part of the debate can be attributed to purely emotional factors (Walker de Felix, 1981), the crux of the problem has to do with the lack of replicable studies on the effectiveness of bilingual education programs over other kinds of special instruction for LEP children. The fact is that many of the early studies lacked a conceptual framework for explaining why or how bilingual education worked, leaving the interpretation of results open to advocates of both sides of the debate.

Several years ago, Jim Cummins (1981) presented a paper entitled 'Wanted: A Theoretical Framework for Relating Language Proficiency to Academic Achievement among Bilingual Students'. In this paper, Cummins outlined a conceptual framework for bilingual schooling based upon the transfer of cognitive/academic skills developed in the student's native language to dominant language of the school. A by-product of Cummins' work was the call for more theoretically based research in bilingual education as a means to build. a stronger case for effective bilingual programs.

A theoretically based framework enables researchers to draw upon previous literature for both the design and interpretation of new studies. Moreover, it provides the readers of research with a more complete picture of how a particular study addressed a problem predicted by the framework. Without a theoretical base, it is virtually impossible to compare and contrast studies concerning the effectiveness of bilingual programs. For example, a recent Government Accounting Agency (GAO) report (1987) on the achievement of LEP students served by bilingual programs compared to LEP students who were schooled in regular classrooms found that students in bilingual programs did better than their counterparts in non-bilingual programs. This finding, unfortunately, was based upon a simplistic voting system which did not differentiate among the various kinds of bilingual programs. A more basic flaw of the report, however, was that it did not adhere to a conceptual framework for deciding which programs to include in the bilingual sample, so that the results are essentially meaningless.

An even worse example is explained by Willig (1987) and Secada (1987). Baker (1987) and Baker & de Kanter (1981, 1983) are considered some of the most powerful antibilingual education studies because of Baker's ties to federal policymakers. Baker's work consistently fails to adhere to conceptual frameworks in the literature. He even fails to maintain consistent definitions of programs, such as immersion, as he compares and contrasts results of early bilingual programs.

As such, Baker's work can be compared to Coleman et al.'s (1966) research. As noted researcher Pedhauzer (1982) points out, Coleman's failure to rely on established theoretical educational frameworks led to expensive and misguided governmental policies to educational practices. Additionally, his work tended to blame the victim of poor education so that even today practitioners continue to describe children's school failures in terms of their poor home environments, as Coleman had. Pedhauzer noted that although the Coleman Report made important contributions to educational and social scientific research, it had many critics. Its worse criticism is the absence of a theory to guide the analysis. 'In sum, the questions posed explicitly or implicitly by Coleman and his associates regarding the process of achievement cannot be answered in the absence of a theoretical model about the relations among the variables under study' (p. 193).

Another important reason for relying on a theoretical framework has to do with how to carry out solid research in relatively hostile environments. Many school districts, for instance, have not allowed bilingual researchers to conduct studies in their schools out of fear of litigation: How could they allow an experimental-control design under the Lau guidelines (Lau v. Nichols, 1974)? One way to address this problem is change the research question, a solution pointed out by Christina Bratt Paulson (1980) nearly ten years ago. Rather than the question 'Is bilingual education effective?', a more appropriate question for future studies is 'How is bilingual education effective?' This perspective moves researchers away from comparing achievement results of bilingual education programs with those of other kinds of special programs for LEP students, and instead asks them to investigate what works within bilingual programs having a theoretical basis for their implementation.

Exemplary studies

What is generally lacking in bilingual education is a prescription for teachers who wish to lead an effective bilingual classroom. Recent studies funded by the Department of Education, however, shed some light on what the effective bilingual education classroom looks like.

For example, Tikunoff and his associates at the Far West Laboratory (Tikunoff & Vazquez-Faria, 1982) designed a massive study to examine effective teaching practices in bilingual classrooms in six sites throughout the United States. This study was driven by a theoretical framework of effective teaching behaviors found in the general literature on teaching and learning.

They found that

1. Limited English proficient (LEP) students in effective classrooms spent 3/4 of their day engaged in basic skills instruction.
2. Effective bilingual teachers used those teaching behaviors that elicit productive participation of students in completing instructional tasks.
3. Effective bilingual teachers used small group instruction and whole group instruction almost equally.
4. Bilingual teachers' dual language skills allowed the teachers to integrate students who arrived throughout the year. By May all students were succeeding, in spite of numerous students arriving late in the year.
5. Teachers used the mother tongue and culture of the students.
6. Effective teachers also developed both the native language and English to help students with the transition into the English-only program.

As Tikunoff noted, however, the sites surveyed determined who the effective teachers were that the researchers saw. This method of identifying schools adds a highly subjective element to the study. A second subjective factor in the study can be seen in statements such as, 'alternating between the two languages whenever necessary to ensure clarity of instruction for LEP students' (Tikunoff, 1985: 3). Without additional information, it is unlikely that researchers could determine through observation alone when a switch was 'necessary' for effective teaching.

Phase II of Tikunoff's (1985) study is extremely valuable because in it he attempted to verify the findings of Phase I. This practice is especially necessary in bilingual education where sociolinguistic realities can vary by neighborhood, generation, and specific language. The generalizability, stability, utility, and compatibility between the findings of other studies and his initial phase needed to be verified. Five researchers, including Lily Wong Fillmore, presented papers on the compatibility issue; reports are included in Tikunoff (1985).

In her own Department of Education study, Wong Fillmore (1982) investigated bilingual classrooms from a theoretical framework based on language use. She noted that the type of instructional programs that LEPs are exposed to affects their English language acquisition. Observers were in each classroom everyday of the school year. They tape recorded children to document the opportunities that existed in each classroom for language learning. The observations were both formal and informal. Formally, each child was observed during a major learning activity in that class for thirty minutes each month. Audio recordings and detailed notes were then reviewed by the researchers, who reconstructed the events to establish what 'seems to make sense or not make sense to language learners' (p. 288). Additionally, four subjects in each class were observed all day with a video camera recording all interactions. Informally, observers noted interactions that facilitated or hindered language learning.

The researchers found a great deal of variation among the four classrooms they studied, an unexpected result. The differences they encountered could not be attributed to the linguistic or cultural backgrounds of the students. 'Instead, the differences appear to stem from the way language was used in each of the four classrooms and this, in large part, was affected by the way each was organized for instruction' (p. 290).

Linguistically isolated children interacting in their native language failed to learn English as quickly as children in linguistically mixed classrooms that provided lots of contact with English speaking children and teachers. On the other hand, 'where a range of language proficiency is present among the students, the instructional situation is harder to manage' (Wong Fillmore, 1982: 293).

Wong Fillmore found that the best language learning situations were those classrooms where children were grouped by language ability for instruction but where both languages were used as mediums of instruction. Also the children had opportunities for informal language development from their English-speaking peers. Significantly, the teacher was an active instructor who kept the two languages separate without translating across languages, directed instruction even when children were working in small groups, and monitored children's responses in large as well as small groupwork.

Again, while the study provides some guidelines for practitioners, many questions are left unanswered concerning the distribution of language for bilingual instruction: Was one language more effective to express praise or for conceptual development? Were teachers who were effective users of language cognizant of language use? Did they plan for language use or did they intuit which language to use when?

Criticism of current bilingual research

The kinds of studies described above have contributed a great deal of useful knowledge on classroom practices that promote linguistic and academic growth among LEP students. A major problem with most studies of bilingual education remains, however, and that is that they fail to provide guidelines that teachers can use in their daily experiences.

One common reason for the absence of transportable guidelines is that research conducted in classrooms, wonderful and messy as they are, is frequently subjective. Authors present information that justifies their biases, they select variables important to them, or allow personal subjectivity to enter in other ways. This means that the program—even if successful—will be incapable of being replicated in other classrooms. In other words, subjective measures of classroom practices may be little better than not looking into classroom practices at all. Small wonder that noted educational researcher Herbert Walberg discounted the bilingual education research in the GAO report because the studies were all conducted by proponents of dual language use. As Walberg explained, 'What would be best for all concerned, especially the children, would be independent and rigorous experimentation on the results of such programs' (GAO, 1987: 72).

One way to conduct rigorous research in bilingual education that would be useful for practitioners would be to pay more attention to what actually occurs in schools—not only the classrooms, but the hallways, the lunchrooms, the playgrounds, and bus stops as well. Since wide-ranging studies are impractical, verification with other sites, replication, and other educational research practices can expand the research findings.

There is a large gap in our literature regarding a description of the classroom practices in the effective programs. For example, when did teachers use the native language? Was the native language used for social comments, commands, or higher order questions? Did teachers develop English language skills systematically? Were they good teachers by standards established in the effective classroom literature?

Effective English as a Second Language classrooms

The literature on effective English as a second language (ESL) classrooms is even sketchier than bilingual classroom research, probably because those programs are seldom scrutinized by the public with the same vigor bilingual programs are.

The U.S. Department of Education currently seems to favor some sort of immersion education as the model program for ESL instruction. Hernandez-Chavez (1984) has pointed out, however, that immersion education is entirely inadequate for language minority children in the United States. Immersion education assumes that children who enter the program will continue to develop their native language, a necessary ingredient for success. In fact, the native language of the minority child is often non-standard, and therefore subject to denigration and ridicule by school personnel. Moreover, Wallace Lambert, the psychologist who was involved in the first French immersion program in Canada, adamantly opposes the use of immersion education except for upper middle class students with well developed cognitive skills in their native language (Lambert, 1984).

Again the debate over the effectiveness of one kind of program over another is fueled by the lack of research findings. There are simply too many unanswered questions: What goes on in immersion classrooms? What are the background variables that interact with achievement in immersion classrooms? Are ESL pullout programs teaching the same kinds of information as immersion programs? To what extent are ESL students interacting in their native language? To give an indication of how little is known about language use in immersion programs, a researcher comparing bilingual with immersion classrooms in a major urban school district privately confessed that some immersion program teachers in that study were using more Spanish than bilingual teachers in a comparison group.

Much ESL classroom literature is of the how-to nature. Some of it seems very helpful. For instance, Enright & McCloskey (1985) describe a communicative classroom, including activities and floor plans. The model, based on the observation of summer school classes, has not been tested empirically in more typical settings, however, and some of it contradicts both effective bilingual class studies cited previously.

Chamot & O'Malley (1986) have produced an exciting program elaborating on Cummins' (1981) theoretical framework and the movement of ESL teaching in content area instruction (Mohan, 1986). The program is designed for LEP students who are being prepared for mainstream content area instruction. In the Cognitive Academic Language Learning Approach upper elementary and secondary students are taught to use learning strategies to assist the development of language and content area concepts. This program focuses on the cognitive task of learning a new language for use in school content areas. In math, for example, middle school students use English to solve problems and add math concepts appropriate to their grade level. They do not count and do simple arithmetic, as in traditional ESL programs. Studies show that by developing learning strategies, students can become more effective learners (O'Malley, 1985).

In spite of its promise, there are two significant problems with Chamot and O'Malley's work that deserve consideration. One is their early assertion that there is no time in ESL programs to develop the affective dimension. In a subsequent article (1987), they include affective needs under social-affective learning strategies, which are defined as the interaction with another person to aid learning, as in cooperation or asking questions for clarification or the use of some kind of affective control to assist learning. Examples of social-affective strategies include (a) eliciting from a teacher or peer additional explanation, (b) working together with peers to solve a problem, and (c) reducing anxiety by using mental techniques that make one feel competent to do the task.

The role of affect in a skills-based program needs further study, however. As Acton & Walker de Felix (1986) have contended, the affective domain is always involved in second language learning. They cite a number of scholars to demonstrate that a sense of well-being in the new language will only develop with greater second language skills. The affective and cognitive domains are inextricably intertwined as the student goes through the socialization process to become a member of the second language learning community. According to this perspective, student participation in the content area ESL activities will probably be enhanced, and learning increased, if a wide range of students' emotional needs are met, especially until the time that the students' new language identity is established.

The second problem ignored by Chamot and O'Malley and other advocates of ESL in the content areas has to do with ESL teacher preparation. As Sanchez & Walker de Felix (1986) have demonstrated, a district's weakest teachers may be assigned to classrooms with LEP children. Ineffective teachers can contribute to validity threats due to differential time spent on the treatment, lack of praise and other affective factors, and general organizational problems. These threats, if not specifically studied, should at least be controlled in a study.

Research that takes into account effective classroom practices associated with any ESL approach is sorely needed. Richards (1987) suggests that until ESL researchers expand their interests from only building models based on research to educating effective teachers, the level of professionalism of ESL educators will continue to be questioned.

While there has been an expansion of the theoretical concepts, research issues, and subject matter content which constitute much of the field, few who are engaged in developing this knowledge base or research agenda would claim any direct relation between their work and the preparation of language teachers ... While there is a body of practice in teacher education in TESOL—based almost exclusively on intuition and common sense—until recently there has been little systematic study of second language teaching processes which could provide a theoretical basis for deriving practices in TESOL teacher education (p. 210).

The Stallings Observation Instrument

A good starting point for ESL researchers and teachers alike is to learn how to systematically observe what goes on in classrooms where there are language minority children present. The Stallings Observation Instrument (SOI) is an effective tool for providing teachers with objective classroom data. Stallings & Stipek (1986) describe several studies conducted with this particular method of systematic observation in the third edition of the *Handbook of Research on Teaching*.

As a classroom observation instrument, the SOI has a high reliability index of between 0.8 and 0.9 on interrater reliability. In essence, the SOI consists of two components, the Snapshot and the Five Minute Interval (FMI). During the Snapshot, the observer notes and codes the teacher's action, moves his/her eyes clockwise around the room and notes what all students are doing, and then codes the actions on a coding sheet.

During the FMI, the observer focuses exclusively on the teacher. The observer codes the teacher's interactions with aides or other adults and visitors or with students. The interactions with students are divided among whole class, large group (11, one less than the whole group), small group (2–10), and individual. Additionally, the individual student is coded for initial interaction and/or continuing interaction.

The observation is carried out at the same time each day for three consecutive days. If an interruption occurs and the teacher is out of the classroom longer than five minutes, that observation is invalidated and three more consecutive days must be scheduled.

The coded material is edited, optically scanned, then analyzed by computer. A printout profile of the teacher gives information as to the types of instruction observed and the amount of time students were on task. Beside the teacher's profile are recommended percentages of each activity based on research on effective teaching. For example, the literature is quite clear that a teacher who spends more than 15% of a class attending to managerial tasks probably cannot be considered an effective instructor.

Not only is the SOI objective, it is also the only major instrument to take into consideration the language of the interaction. Of major concern to educators of LEPs is the amount and condition of native language use. Using the SOI, observers fluent in English and the native language note who used which language under what conditions. Researchers can then determine if the mother tongue is used for socializing, organizing, academic work, simple commands, or higher order questions. The use of English can likewise be documented and use of the two languages compared. The instrument can also be modified to meet particular research needs.

Time and LEP students

In addition to language use, use of time in a classroom is an important consideration. Cummins (1981) argued that on the average LEP children need two to three years to learn basic communication skills in the school language but five to seven years to learn to do cognitively demanding work such as achievement tests. Most districts do not allow children to remain in language development programs longer than three years. Many studies have shown that LEP children constitute a high percentage of the low achievers and school dropouts.

Levin, Libman & Amaid (1980) demonstrated that low achievers were actively involved in instruction only 50% of the time, as compared to 70% involvement among high achievers. If LEP children receive as little instruction as the low-achieving children in the Levin *et al.* study, it is no wonder they need five to seven years to achieve on cognitively demanding tasks. In one of the earliest studies on time in the classroom, Fisher *et al.* (1978) found that although students attended school 5.4 to 6.8 hours per day and an average of 4.75 hours per day were allocated for instruction, actual instruction occurred only two to four hours per day.

In another early study, Stallings *et al.* (1979) described the effective secondary reading classroom as having more interactive instruction and actively monitored seatwork, and students on task more than average classes.

Time spent on a particular task has been shown to be less important than the amount of time students spend engaged in academic tasks (Walberg, Schiller & Haertel, 1979). Evertson & Emmer (1982) and Stallings (1980) demonstrated that the amount of student–teacher interaction is also positively associated with student task engagement. This interaction is particularly important for second language development (Wong Fillmore, 1983).

Several researchers have demonstrated that the time teachers spend interacting with students is positively related to all learning (Evertson & Emmer, 1982; Fisher *et al.*, 1978; Stallings, 1980). Stallings (1981) found greater achievement gains in those classrooms that incorporated more interactive instruction and more activities per class.

Suggested future research

The trends in objective classroom research provide an important theoretical framework to study the effects of various language-use paradigms in programs for LEP students. For example, objective studies in bilingual programs could answer questions regarding the amount of time needed in each language, given specific background variables such as student proficiency in each language, age, and sociolinguistic characteristics of the community.

Studies are needed to test the effects of extant models of language use. Jacobson's code-switching concurrent model (Jacobson, this volume), for example, is effective for teacher training. It provides a structured approach by helping bilingual teachers keep the languages separate, a factor Wong Fillmore (1982) stressed as crucial to second language development. The approach must be varied, however, depending on the language abilities of the students. Recently arrived immigrants, for example, cannot take part in cognitively demanding, context embedded lessons in English.

Teachers need the structure of the code-switching approach or other prescriptive guidelines because fluent teachers are frequently unaware of their language choice. Teachers who are less proficient in one language, the normal case in bilingualism, may favor their more proficient language. Worse, they may overuse the less proficient language in an attempt to develop their own proficiency without considering the needs of the students.

In addition, with the current pressures on teachers to meet state and district prescriptions of basic skills, it stands to reason that language use will remain a great contingency factor. Undoubtedly the development of the basic skills (usually in English) will receive teachers' major attention. While experienced, linguistically sophisticated teachers may successfully attend to appropriate use of both languages, inexperienced teachers may not have sufficient data to even consider language use in their teaching. Since the literature on effective bilingual classrooms conducted by Tikunoff, Wong Fillmore, Jacobson and others is so clear on the importance of language use, specific guidelines for that language use may be the single most important factor emerging from future research in bilingual/ESL education.

Also continued research is necessary to build on sociolinguistic theoretical frameworks regarding home language use and prestige factors. Wong Fillmore (1987) noted that students who learn a different language at school may not be able to communicate with their family. This break in communication can lead to identity problems and alienation. Most literature on school dropouts notes the lack of affiliation of most dropouts. Could this be attributed to lack of a strong familial and ethnic identity precipitated by school language use policies?

Similarly Cummins (1986) demonstrated how the gap between school and home culture can lead to students being debilitated because they lack a sense of self-efficacy. Olson's (1987) dissertation seemed to corroborate this. Reanalyzing data from the National Assessment Evaluation Project, she found that adding ethnic or cultural heritage to any programs for LEPs increased their academic achievement.

Concern for effective programs for LEP students has led to the implementation of a wide variety of programs called bilingual/ESL education. Important studies from both an effective classroom perspective and from a language use perspective have led to a solid theoretical framework on which future research should build.

References

ACTON, W.R. and WALKER DE FELIX, J. 1986, Acculturation and mind. In J. M. VALDES (ed.), *Culture Bound: Bridging the Cultural Gap in Language Teaching* (pp. 20–32). New York: Cambridge University Press.

BAKER, K. 1987, Comment on Willig's 'A meta-analysis of selected studies in the effectiveness of bilingual education.' *Review of Educational Research* 57, 3, 351–62.

BAKER, K. and DE KANTER, A. 1981, *Effectiveness of Bilingual Education: A Review of the Literature*. Washington, DC: US Department of Education.

BAKER, K. and DE KANTER, A. (eds) 1983, *Bilingual Education: A Reappraisal of Federal Policy*. Lexington, MA: Lexington Books.

CHAMOT, A.U. and O'MALLEY, J.M. 1986, *A Cognitive Academic Language Learning Approach: An ESL Content-Based Curriculum*. Wheaton, MD: National Clearinghouse for Bilingual Education.

—— 1987, The cognitive academic language learning approach: A bridge to the mainstream. *TESOL Quarterly* 21(2), 227–49.

COLEMAN, J.S., CAMPBELL, E.Q., HOBSON, C.J., MCPARTLAND, J., MOOD, A.M., WEINFELD, F.D. and YORK, R.L. 1966, *Equality of Educational Opportunity*. Washington DC: US Government Printing Office.

CUMMINS, J. 1981, The role of primary development in promoting educational success for language minority students. In *Schooling and Language Minority Students: A Theoretical Framework*. Los Angeles, CA: Evaluation, Dissemination, and Assessment Center, California State University, Los Angeles.

—— 1986, Empowering minority students: A framework for intervention. *Harvard Educational Review* 56(1), 18–36.

ENRIGHT, D.S. and MCCLOSKEY, M.L. 1985, Yes, talking!: Organizing the classroom to promote second language acquisition. *TESOL Quarterly* 19(3), 431–53.

EVERTSON, C. and EMMER, E. 1982, Effective management at the beginning of the school year in junior high classes. *Journal of Educational Psychology* 74, 485–98.

FISHER, C.W., FILBY, N.N., MARLIAVE, R.S., CAHEN, L.S., DISHAW, M.M., MOORE, J.E. and BERLINER, D.C. 1978, *Teaching Behaviors, Academic Learning Time, and Student Achievement: Final Report of Phase III-B, Beginning Teacher Evaluation Study*. San Francisco: Far West Laboratory for Education Research and Development.

GOVERNMENT ACCOUNTING AGENCY 1987, *Bilingual Education: A New Look at the Research Evidence*. Washington, DC: US Government Printing Office.

HAKUTA, K. 1986, *Mirror of Language*. New York: Basic Books.

HERNANDEZ-CHAVEZ, E. 1984, The inadequacy of English immersion education as an educational approach for language minority students in the United States. In California State Department of Education (ed.), *Studies on Immersion Education: A Collection for United States Educators* (pp. 144–183). Sacramento, CA: Author.

LAMBERT, W. 1984, An overview of issues in immersion education. In California State Department of Education (ed.), *Studies on Immersion Education: A Collection for United States Educators* (pp. 8–30). Sacramento, CA: Author.

LEVIN, T., LIBMAN, Z. and AMIAD, R. 1980, Behavioral patterns of students under an individualized learning strategy. *Instructional Science* 9, 85–100.

LAU V. NICHOLS, 414 US 563 (1974).

MOHAN, B.A. 1986, *Language and Content*. Reading, MA: Addison-Wesley.

OLSON, S. 1987, The long-term academic effects of bilingual education programs on a national sample of Mexican-American sophomores: A component analysis. Unpublished Doctoral Dissertation, University of Houston, Houston, TX.

O'MALLEY, J.M. 1985, Learning strategy applications to content instruction in second language development. In *Issues in English Language Development*. Wheaton, MD: National Clearinghouse for Bilingual Education.

PAULSTON, C.B. 1980, *Bilingual Education: Theories and Issues*. Rowley, MA: Newbury House.

PEDHAUZER, E.J. 1982, *Multiple Regression in Behavioral Research*. New York: Holt.

RICHARDS, J.C. 1987, The dilemma of teacher education in TESOL. *TESOL Quarterly* 21(2), 209–26.

SANCHEZ, K. and WALKER DE FELIX, J. 1986, Second language teachers' abilities: Some equity concerns. *Journal of Educational Equity Leadership* 6(4), 313–21.

SECADA, W.G. 1987, This is 1987, not 1980: A comment on a comment. *Review of Educational Research* 57(3), 377–84.

STALLINGS, J.A. 1980, Allocated academic learning time revisited, or beyond time on task. *Educational Researcher* 9(11), 11–16.

—— 1981, *Testing Teachers' In-Class Instruction and Measuring Change Resulting from Staff Development*. Princeton, NJ: National Teacher Examinations Policy Council.

STALLINGS, J.A., CORY, R., FAIRWEATHER, J. and NEEDELS, M. 1979, *Early Childhood Education Classroom Evaluation* (Final Report for Department of Education, State of California). Menlo Park, CA: SRI International.

STALLINGS, J.A. and STIPEK, D. 1986, Research on early childhood and elementary school programs. In M. WITTROCK (ed.), *Handbook of Research on Teaching* (3rd edn) (pp. 727–54). New York: Macmillan.

TIKUNOFF, W.J. 1985, *Developing Student Functional Proficiency for LEP Students*. Portland, OR: Northwest Regional Educational Laboratory.

TIKUNOFF, W. and VAZQUEZ-FARIA, J. 1982, Components of effective instruction for NES/LES students. In *Consequences for Students in Successful Bilingual Instructional Settings*. Part I of the Study Report, Vol. V, edited by W. TIKUNOFF, 15–26. San Francisco, CA: Far West Laboratory for Educational Research and Development.

TROIKE, R.C. 1978, Research evidence for the effectiveness of bilingual education. *NABE Journal* 3(1).

WALBERG, H.J., SCHILLER, D. and HAERTEL, G.D. 1979, The quiet revolution in educational research. *Phi Delta Kappan* 61(3), 179–182.

WALKER DE FELIX, J. 1981, Who's afraid of bilingual education? *Journal of the Texas Association for Bilingual Education* (December), 18–21.

WILLIG, A.C. 1985, A meta-analysis of selected studies on the effectiveness of bilingual education. *Review of Educational Research* 55, 269–317.

—— 1987, Examining bilingual educational research through meta-analysis and negative review: A response to Baher. *Review of Educational Research* 57, 3, 363–76.

WONG FILLMORE, L. 1982, Instructional language as linguistic input: Second language learning in classrooms. In L.C. WILKINSON (ed.), *Communicating in the Classroom*. New York: Academic Press.

—— 1983, Effective language use in bilingual classrooms. In W.J. TIKUNOFF (ed.), *Compatibility of the SBIF Features with Other Research on Instruction for Limited English Proficient Students*, 43–61. San Francisco, CA: Far West Laboratory for Educational Research and Development.

—— 1987, Instructional planning for linguistic development. Paper Presented at the Meeting of the Texas Education Agency, Austin, TX.

3 Integrating language and content: Implications for language distribution in bilingual classrooms

ROBERT D. MILK

A commonly observed phenomenon in bilingual communities throughout the United States, particularly in recent years, has been a tendency for non-English mother tongues, when left unattended, to be replaced over time by English as schoolchildren proceed through school. The sociolinguistic forces that support this shift have been amply documented (Penalosa, 1980; Ramirez, 1985), and it appears that bilingual programs which purport to be sociolinguistically based, and which have as a goal dual language development, have taken great care to develop program strategies that might take into account these external forces (Cohen, 1975; Jacobson, 1981).

Discussions on sociolinguistic relevance of programs for language minority children have often focused on language attitudes, on the different language varieties present in the community, and on language use patterns outside the classroom. These are all important contextual variables that need to be taken into account when designing and implementing bilingual programs. Of equal importance, and perhaps more immediate relevance to the classroom teacher, is a specific concern focusing on the extent to which language use patterns of children and teachers *within the classroom* might support (or not support) the primary goals of the school (Shultz, 1975; Milk, 1982). In considering instructional design, consequently, the focus of many discussions, particularly those concerned with bilingual methodology, has been on the issue of language distribution within individual classrooms (Jacobson, 1981; Ovando & Collier, 1985).

Clearly, issues related to language distribution must be at the heart of any substantive discussion of bilingual methodology, for there is no more fundamental decision to be made by a bilingual teacher than which language(s) to use when (i.e. with which subjects), and in what manner (i.e. concurrently or following a strict separation of codes). Issues related to language distribution will never be, however, strictly pedagogical, since alternative strategies are deeply dependent on program goals, and program goals are invariably tied to political processes taking place within each school district. Indeed, few decisions are more directly tied in to underlying philosophical orientations towards cultural adaptation and linguistic assimilation than those related to language distribution. [1]

Sociolinguistically oriented discussions of the language distribution issue have recognized the erroneous assumption commonly made that if the second language is heavily stressed in the school environment, the native language will take care of itself in the home and community environment. While this may well be the case in certain sociolinguistic contexts (for example, Anglophone children in Canada), it is clearly not the case for language minority children in the United States (Dolson, 1985; Hernandez-Chavez, 1984). Consequently, for programs in this latter environment where dual language development is a goal, a sociolinguistically based strategy would need to stress development of the language which is in danger of being replaced.

These general principles are widely understood by language education professionals in the late 1980s. The validity of these sociolinguistically oriented arguments for native language support have not changed over the past decade. What *has* changed, at least in the U.S., is both the political reality within which programs operate (with generally less commitment to dual language development as an important outcome goal), as well as the knowledge base undergirding discussions on bilingual methodology. Indeed, so profound have been advancements in the state of knowledge and research related to various aspects of bilingual teaching that it is no longer adequate to frame discussions on language distribution solely with reference to the relative number of minutes that should be allocated for each language, nor in terms of which subject matter areas should be assigned to which language. The reasons for this increasing complexity of issues are threefold:

1. Research on effective bilingual teaching practices are stressing the need to focus primarily on concept development and learning outcomes following integrative practices. Shifting the focus from 'Which language should I use?' to 'How can learning best be achieved?' certainly places language distribution issues in a new light.

2. Research in the area of second language acquisition has made us aware of the need to place greater importance on qualitative aspects of classroom interaction, with a corresponding decrease in emphasis on strictly quantitative analyses (such as typically reflected in studies where the prime concern is determining how much 'exposure' students have to each language of the classroom).

3. The changing nature of ESL methods within bilingual education, with a move away from isolated grammar-based instruction towards more integrative content-based approaches, presents a new dimension to discussions on language distribution that cannot be overlooked.

I will discuss each one of these developments separately.

Integrating language and content in bilingual instruction

There can be no more fundamental question for bilingual methodology than the simple question: 'What characterizes effective bilingual instruction?' In a massive study that grew out of funding generated by Part C of the 1978 amendments to the Bilingual Education Act of 1978, this question was addressed at a number of different sites across the country where bilingual programs had been functioning for a number of years. Following a procedure that involved first identifying successful bilingual classrooms, then investigating closely the features that characterized the instruction in those classrooms, researchers identified a number of 'significant bilingual instructional features' that appeared regularly in these settings, including: (1) use of 'active teaching' behaviors; (2) both responding to and actively using 'cultural referents' from the LEP students' home culture during instruction; (3) use of two languages to mediate instruction; and (4) integration of English language development with regular in-class instruction (Tikunoff, 1983).

These findings can be roughly paraphrased to state that effective bilingual instruction appears to involve active teaching that is culturally relevant, that integrates language development with concept development, and that utilizes fully the two languages of the classroom. These findings are not surprising to those who have observed quality bilingual instruction in action. The active involvement of students in the learning process, with a high frequency of on-task behavior for students, characterizes effective teaching generally, and there is no reason why this should be any different in a bilingual classroom. Moreover, the Deweyan concept of commencing instruction where the learner is demands that we utilize fully the resources that a pupil brings to the task; for language minority children this means drawing on their primary language and their home culture during instruction.

The only one of the four features which, while by no means a novel idea, may surprise some practitioners is the final one listed: integration of English language development with regular in-class instruction. As noted, this is not a new idea, for advocates of bilingual education have argued for years that use of a language as a medium of instruction is one of the best ways to develop and extend a learner's proficiency in that language. The highlighting of this feature, nevertheless, flies in the face of common practice in bilingual education, where 'language development' and 'subject matter development' have often been treated separately, both in the minds of teachers as well as curriculum developers. There are clearly reasonable administrative reasons for this state of affairs. Principals and supervisors are responsible for ensuring that pupils are receiving a balanced curriculum, and that state guidelines for curriculum emphases are being adequately followed. Within bilingual programs, this typically means that the number of minutes per week spent on each of the content areas (including language arts) as well as on the ESL component must be carefully monitored and documented. These procedural concerns, focusing as they do on the separate, discrete identity of each element in the curriculum, clearly fail to encourage instructional practices that might lead to greater integration of language and content development. This does not, of course, mean that creative teachers and supervisors who are aware of the potential for language development during content area instruction cannot find the means for pursuing this strategy; it merely means that administrative concerns and common supervisory procedures fail to encourage the kind of thinking on the part of the teachers that would encourage this outcome.[2]

In addition to practical administrative concerns, there are other reasons why language and content have tended to be dealt with separately. Because of the historical context within which bilingual programs have emerged in the U.S. over the past two decades, as well as the political context within which they operate, methodological issues have often revolved around a rather simplistic consideration of language choice and language distribution within the classroom. Simply stated, the key question has often ended up being nothing more than, 'Which language should I use at this time during the day?' With most legislation focusing heavily on language proficiency as the key criterion for entry and exit into bilingual programs, it is not surprising that the focus of practitioners should be so heavily directed at this consideration (Cummins, 1980). What is often lost sight of, however, is that the ultimate outcome of bilingual programs must necessarily be school achievement, and that language development is only part of this desired outcome.

There is some evidence that integrating language development with concept development may lead to better outcomes in both areas (Friedman, 1985; DeAvila, 1985). Indeed, one study examining the implementation of a curriculum that focused heavily on cognitive development goals without regard to language, found, nevertheless, important gains in language proficiency taking place (Wilson, DeAvila & Intili, 1982).

This is not to say that language development may be ignored since it will likely 'take care of itself'; rather, the point is that the kind of language proficiency that schools should be focusing on can best be developed in the context of regular academic learning and not through lessons where language development is the prime focus of attention. Following Cummins (1984), the kind of language proficiency that is needed by students in order to advance successfully in school, particularly once they reach the upper elementary grades, is one which requires them to do cognitively demanding tasks within conditions that become increasingly context-reduced as they become increasingly proficient in the language(s) of the classroom.

One of the possible implications of this point for language distribution strategies is that, while strict separation of codes may be desirable during language arts instruction, concurrent language use may provide an effective means through which language and content can become successfully integrated in the course of regular academic instruction, *provided that certain conditions are met*. What these conditions are can best be explained in reference to research that focuses on second language acquisition within classroom settings.

Second language acquisition in classroom settings

As a first step in discussing language distribution issues within bilingual programs, it has been necessary to collect data that provide a sense of typical language use patterns in classrooms where bilingual teaching is taking place. Based on studies that have been conducted in this area, some patterns have been commonly observed: (a) English appears to predominate as the primary classroom language in most U.S. bilingual programs (Wong Fillmore, 1986; Ramirez, 1985). This is true even in classrooms where a balanced distribution of the two languages is a stated goal (Shultz, 1975). Many factors contribute to this phenomenon, including transitional goals for programs, teacher preferences due to their own relative language proficiency, administrative pressures, and, not insignificantly, sociolinguistic conditions favoring use of the majority language of the society. (b) In bilingual classrooms where the primary mode of organization involves homogeneous grouping based on language dominance, relatively little communication appears to occur between students in the weaker language (Milk, 1980).

The kind of information provided by these studies on language use patterns in bilingual classrooms has been necessary in order to develop informed guidelines on language distribution for these programs. Because of recent developments within second language acquisition theory, however, the kind of information obtained in many of these studies is no longer adequate for properly addressing the full range of issues raised by bilingual methodology, in particular those questions related to the development of a weaker language as an outcome of bilingual instruction.

An underlying assumption of descriptive studies on language use patterns in bilingual classrooms has been that, in order for language development to occur, there must be significant exposure to the target language. This assumption appears reasonable on the surface, but it is open to misinterpretation depending on what is meant by 'significant exposure'. From a strictly quantitative perspective, what has typically been referred to is 'number of minutes', or else some linguistic measure such as T-units or lexical counts. From the perspective of current second language acquisition theory, however, it is quite possible for an individual to have abundant exposure to a language, yet not acquire it. Among the conditions that must apparently be met in order for acquisition to take place is one which requires the learner to be engaged in some type of social interaction that involves negotiation of meaning.

Based on observations drawn from numerous second language acquisition studies, Long (1981) argues that input factors should be separated from interaction factors in developing a theory of second language acquisition. Input factors include features related to language form (such as syntactic complexity or frequency of nouns and verbs), whereas interaction factors include features related to negotiation of meaning during social interactions (such as comprehension checks, clarification requests, expansions, and restatements). Long states that these factors need to be considered separately since it is possible to modify one without modifying the other, then goes on to argue that it is modified interaction, not modified input that facilitates second language acquisition.

If Long is correct, whenever our focus is on language development in bilingual classrooms, then what needs to be examined in terms of bilingual students' language use is not solely to what extent they are exposed to Language X or Language Y, but rather to what extent they are engaged in meaningful social interactions in that language. Moreover, when the focus is on second language development (as it is, for example, when considering the English of LEP children), the question becomes less one of, 'How many minutes of English is the child exposed to per day or per week?', than one of, 'How can we maximize the opportunities for students to engage in conversations where a true two-way exchange is taking place?' (Ellis, 1985; Hatch, 1983; 152–187).[3]

Clearly, these developments within second language acquisition research cannot be overlooked when discussing language distribution guidelines, no matter how much they add to the complexity of these issues. A full discussion of language distribution issues in bilingual classrooms can no longer be adequately dealt with through reference solely to the 'how much English' vs. 'how much native language' debate. What becomes increasingly clear is that, more important than 'how much' each language is used, is the question of in what manner and in what context each language is used, and what kinds of interactions students are involved in when using the language. For what seems to generate development of a learner's inter-language is not simply exposure to language, but rather involvement in interactions through which a negotiation of meaning is required dealing with matters that are of immediate and direct relevance to the learner.

From this, it is possible to begin to describe ideal contexts for second language acquisition in a bilingual classroom. Consider two key questions related to this: (1) What concerns are of immediate relevance to a learner in a classroom? Clearly, resolving and completing an academic task is of direct relevance to a pupil. (2) What type of classroom context might encourage negotiation of meaning in a weaker language? One possible response might be to place students into groups that are heterogeneous with respect to language proficiency, and to involve them in an academically-based co-operative venture, whereby completion of the task demands interaction within the group. Inevitably, this kind of task-oriented interaction among students at varying proficiency levels will include negotiation of meaning in the weaker language.

The possibilities for integrating language and content are not difficult to perceive in the context of heterogeneous small-group problem-solving sessions involving high levels of peer–peer interaction. But not all classroom learning takes place through small group interaction, and there are times when the teacher will need to be involved in direct instruction to students. In cases where the teacher is developing a lesson in the weaker language of a student, she must necessarily adapt the level of language being used to suit the proficiency level of the student. This, of course, remains the most difficult challenge for attempts to integrate second language development with content development—how to simplify linguistic input and/or interaction without oversimplifying content and without distorting or confusing the message. As Chaudron (1983: 141–142) states, there are highly conflicting demands placed on teachers who are attempting to present academic content in a student's weaker language, for they must 'at the same time present significant and coherent ideas and knowledge, but in a way that is comprehensible to learners who lack fundamental linguistic competence ... The teacher must be careful to be explicit and perspicuous, while meeting the learners' need for linguistic simplicity.' In cases where this is not adequately done by teachers, it can lead to 'ambiguous over-simplification on the one hand, and confusingly redundant over-elaboration on the other' (Chaudron, 1983: 142).

In sum, in light of recent second language acquisition research, it is now necessary to go beyond strictly quantitative questions in order to properly address issues related to language distribution in bilingual classrooms. The key questions related to language distribution must now be framed with regard to relevant qualitative features of classroom interaction that may contribute to the kinds of language development goals that are being sought.

Second language instruction in bilingual education

A third area that cannot be overlooked in examining the changing knowledge base for language distribution issues is that of methodology for second language instruction. Developments in this area have been marked by profound shifts in both theory and practice over the past two decades. There was a time in the early days of Title VII programs when the ESL component in most bilingual programs focused heavily on the development of student mastery over basic structures of the language—i.e. on linguistic competence. The means through which this goal was pursued included a strong reliance on pattern drills drawn from a grammatical syllabus that focused almost exclusively on form, and very little on language functions. Later, under the influence of changing trends in linguistic theory, and guided by the obvious inadequacies of existing methods, many second language teachers came to embrace 'communicative competence' as a primary goal of instruction, leading to techniques that placed much stronger emphasis on communication in the target language and on meaningful interaction among peers in the classroom.

Hence, 'communicative language teaching' evolved in the ESL literature as a viable alternative to structure-based, form-focused approaches to second language instruction. Among ESL professionals most closely linked to bilingual education practice, however, the emergence of communicative competence as the primary goal for ESL instruction was, while an improvement over earlier grammar-based approaches, clearly too limited for fully meeting the needs of limited English proficient (LEP) students. As pointed out by Saville-Troike (1983: 142), LEP students ultimately need to do much more than merely communicate in English—they 'must learn to learn through the medium of English... Developing communicative competence alone is a desirable but insufficient goal for English teaching... We need to develop their *academic competence* [author's emphasis] as well, and this calls for even more changes in our priorities and our procedures.'

The change in priorities for ESL instruction, according to Saville-Troike (1983: 142), includes greater emphasis on vocabulary learning and less on grammar and pronunciation. The change in procedures means no longer teaching English language skills out of context and isolated from subject matter areas. In other words, it includes greater reliance on content-based instruction as a more effective vehicle for developing the full academic competence of LEP students. This call for content-based instruction in ESL, defined as 'a content-based syllabus [that] employs subject-matter content as the point of departure for the language class' (Snow, 1986: 12), will necessarily require greater integration of language and content, as well as closer collaboration between second language instruction and content area instruction. Indeed, as pointed out by Saville-Troike (1985: 118), 'ESL teachers cannot contribute effectively to the development of LEP students' academic competence if the teachers do not know what academic content students are expected to learn.'

Language distribution issues in current perspective

We have examined three areas of knowledge which, due to recent research and evolving theory, seem to be pointing toward the need for greater integration of language and content in bilingual education programs. By the same token, however, this greater integration of language and content has served to obfuscate language distribution issues as conventionally discussed within bilingual methodology. In this final section I wish to explore this final point.

Current discussions on bilingual education in the U.S. have become heavily distorted due, at least in part, to an unfavorable educational climate for the development of languages other than English within the public schools. One example of these distortions is provided by recent interest in immersion programs as an alternative to dual language instruction for LEP children in the U.S. Immersion programs, as implemented in Canada, have always emphasized a two-pronged set of goals: (a) attaining high proficiency levels in a second language; (b) at no expense to achievement in the content areas and development in the first language (Swain, 1985). Unfortunately, some of the discussions on applicability of immersion models for the U.S. have chosen to focus solely on the first goal while ignoring the second. Likewise, discussions on ESL in the content areas, on sheltered English, and on content-based instruction for LEP children, have often been conducted solely in reference to the potential of these approaches for developing the second language (English), but with little attention paid to what may or may not be happening with respect to the students' native language, or to achievement in the content areas. As a consequence, in these discussions, little if any reference is made to language distribution issues, other than to insist on the strict separation of languages. This failure to deal substantively with language distribution issues leaves the unfortunate impression that somehow they are no longer relevant. Nothing could be further from the truth.

The literature on 'sheltered-English' programs, while acknowledging that they are 'components of bilingual education programs' (Curtain, 1986: 9), strongly emphasizes the link between second language acquisition research and some of the salient features of sheltered-English instruction, which include: (a) a focus on meaning rather than form; (b) linguistic modifications such as simplified speech and controlled vocabulary; (c) contextual clues to help convey meaning; (d) conversational interaction, based on subject content, that is interesting and real to the students; (e) allowance for a silent period until students are ready to speak; and (f) careful separation of languages of instruction (Curtain, 1986: 11).

This latter point—strict separation of languages—is an article of faith among many second language teachers. When the primary goal of a class is development of a second language, it would appear to make eminent sense, particularly in contexts where students have few opportunities to use the second language outside of school. However, when the primary goal of instruction in a particular lesson is academic content, including development of higher level concepts and completion of cognitively demanding tasks, prohibition of access to the native language becomes a highly debatable proposition. In these contexts, *not* to discuss language distribution issues is to overlook, if not deny, the relevance of the student's first language in developing cognitively and in achieving at age-appropriate levels academically. Such a position cannot be supported from a research standpoint (Cummins, 1984).

The movement towards integration of language and content appears at times to be accompanied by an underlying disregard or disinterest in continued development of the native language of LEP children. This need not be the case, for as we have seen in recent research, high quality bilingual instruction is typically characterized by just such integration. At the root of the problem appears to be a failure, in many discussions of the issue, to clarify between instructional contexts where the primary goal is second language acquisition, and other contexts where the primary objectives include attainment of content area goals. At the root of this lack of clarity is a failure to carefully consider fundamental language distribution issues, including which language to use when, and in what manner.

The challenge for bilingual educators is to explore ways that we might capitalize on the potential for second language development of content-based approaches without overlooking the integral educational needs of LEP children, which include higher levels of academic achievement accompanied by full development of the first language. Only non-dogmatic empirical research into language distribution issues can fulfil this challenge.

Notes to Chapter 3

1. Direct evidence of this is provided by recent attempts of the Reagan administration to include under Title VII legislation funds for English-only programs, a proposal which has included within it some interesting distortions of existing research evidence (cf. General Accounting Office, 1987).
2. Anecdotally, elementary school teachers report that in some instances they have had lesson plans rejected by their principals when they have attempted to integrate second language instruction into one of the content areas.
3. Answers to the question, 'How can we maximize opportunities for students from different language backgrounds to interact with each other?' must necessarily take into account the influences of language attitudes and of social distance between different ethnolinguistic groups (Johnson, 1980).

References

CHAUDRON, C. 1983, Foreigner talk in the classroom: An aid to learning? In H.W. SELIGER and M.H. LONG (eds), *Classroom-Oriented Research in Second Language Acquisition* (pp. 127–145). Rowley, MA: Newbury House.
COHEN, A. 1975, *A Sociolinguistic Approach to Bilingual Education.* Rowley, MA: Newbury House.

CUMMINS, J. 1980, The entry and exit fallacy in bilingual education. *NABE Journal* 4, 25–60.

—— 1984, *Bilingualism and Special Education: Issues in Assessment and Pedagogy.* Clevedon, England: Multilingual Matters.

CURTAIN, H.A. 1986, Integrating content and language instruction. In K.F. WILLETS (ed.), *Integrating Language and Content Instruction*, ER5 (pp. 9–11). Los Angeles, CA: Center for Language Education and Research, UCLA.

DEAVILA, E. 1985, Science and math: A natural context for language development. In *Delivering Academic Excellence to Culturally Diverse Populations*. Proceedings of Conference Sponsored by Bilingual Education Skills and Training Center of the Peter Sammartino College of Education. Teaneck, NJ: Fairleigh Dickinson University.

DOLSON, D.P. 1985, *The Application of Immersion Education in the United States.* Rosslyn, VA: National Clearinghouse for Bilingual Education.

ELLIS, R. 1985, *Understanding Second Language Acquisition*. Oxford: Oxford University Press.

FRIEDMAN, M. 1985, Teacher education and language development through math and science: New Jersey's response. In *Delivering Academic Excellence to Culturally Diverse Populations*. Proceedings of Conference Sponsored by Bilingual Education Skills and Training Center of the Peter Sammartino College of Education. Teaneck, NJ: Fairleigh Dickinson University.

GENERAL ACCOUNTING OFFICE 1987, Bilingual education: A new look at the research evidence. *Briefing Report to the Chairman, Committee on Education and Labor, House of Representatives*, GAO/PEMD-87–12BR. Washington: General Accounting Office.

HATCH, E.M. 1983, *Psycholinguistics: A Second Language Perspective.* Rowley, MA: Newbury House.

HERNANDEZ-CHAVEZ, E. 1984, The inadequacy of English immersion education as an educational approach for language minority students in the United States. In *Studies on Immersion Education: A Collection for United States Educators* (pp. 144–183). Sacramento, CA: California State Department of Education.

JACOBSON, R. 1981, The implementation of a bilingual instruction model: The new concurrent approach. In R.V. PADILLA (ed.), *Ethnoperspectives in Bilingual Education Research, Vol. 3: Bilingual Education Technology* (pp. 14–29). Ypsilanti, MI: Eastern Michigan University.

JOHNSON, D.M. 1980, Peer tutoring, social interaction and the acquisition of English as a second language by Spanish-speaking elementary school children. Unpublished Ph.D. Dissertation, Stanford University.

LONG, M.H. 1981, Input, interaction, and second language acquisition. In H. WINITZ (ed.), *Annals of the New York Academy of Sciences* 379, 250–78.

MILK, R.D. 1980, Variation in language use patterns across different group settings in two bilingual second grade classrooms. Unpublished Ph.D. Dissertation, Stanford University.

—— 1982, Language use in bilingual classrooms: Two case studies. In M. HINES and W. RUTHERFORD (eds), *On TESOL '81* (pp. 181–191). Washington, DC: Teachers of English to Speakers of Other Languages.

OVANDO, C.J. and COLLIER, V.P. 1985, *Bilingual and ESL Classrooms: Teaching in Multicultural Contexts.* New York: McGraw-Hill Book Company.

PENALOSA, F. 1980, *Chicano Sociolinguistics.* Rowley, MA: Newbury House.

RAMIREZ, A.G. 1985, *Bilingualism through Schooling: Cross-Cultural Education for Minority and Majority Students.* Albany, NY: State University of New York Press.

SAVILLE-TROIKE, M. 1983, Teaching and testing both communicative and academic skills in English as a second language. In S. SEIDNER (ed.), *Issues of Language Assessment, Vol. 2: Language Assessment and Curriculum Planning* (pp. 137–142). Evanston, IL: Illinois State Board of Education.

—— 1985, Training teachers to develop the academic competence of LEP students. *Issues in English Language Development.* Rosslyn, VA: National Clearinghouse for Bilingual Education.

SHULTZ, J. 1975, Language use in bilingual classrooms. Unpublished paper presented at TESOL Conference, Los Angeles, CA.

SNOW, M.A. 1986, *Common Terms in Second Language Education*, ER2. Los Angeles: Center for Language Education and Research, UCLA.

SWAIN, M. 1985, Large-scale communicative language testing: A case study. In Y.P. LEE, A.C. FOK, R. LORD and G. LOW (eds), *New Directions in Language Testing* (pp. 35–46). Oxford: Pergamon Press.

TIKUNOFF, W.J. 1983, Five significant bilingual instructional features. In W.J. TIKUNOFF (ed.), *Compatibility of the SBIF Features with Other Research on Instruction for LEP Students*, SBIF-83-R.9/10 (pp. 5–18). San Francisco: Far West Laboratory.

WILSON, B., DEAVILA, E.A. and INTILI, J.K. 1982, Improving cognitive, linguistic and academic skills in bilingual classrooms. Paper presented at the Annual Meeting of the American Educational Research Association, New York.

WONG FILLMORE, L. 1986, Learning English through bilingual instruction: The issue of variation. Presentation at TESOL Conference, Anaheim, CA.

4 New directions in bilingual research design: The study of interactive decision making

CHRISTIAN FALTIS

Research in bilingual education in the United States has tended to focus on two interrelated instructional variables (Wong Fillmore & Valadez, 1986):

1. The sequencing of language in the content areas.
2. Time allotted for the two languages, both within sequencing and within the curriculum.

One reason that these variables are given so much importance in the research literature is because bilingual education in the United States is overwhelmingly transitional in nature; that is, bilingual instruction is offered only until limited English speaking (LEP) students have acquired enough English to deal with instruction given exclusively in that language (GAO, 1987). Studying the sequencing and time distribution of language enables researchers to better understand the special instructional needs of LEP students within a transitional model of bilingual education. For example, Cummins (1981) has shown that bilingual students perform much better in English-only classrooms when they have developed major content area concepts in their native language and have had at least four years of exposure to English in school. Accordingly, Cummins' work supports the idea that the two languages should be sequenced so that LEP students have the opportunity to develop high levels of native language proficiency before moving entirely into an English-only classroom environment.

Other research has suggested that the most effective time allotment design for transitional bilingual programs is one based upon the notion of balanced usage: 50% English, 50% the students' native language

(Legarreta, 1979) for all content areas except reading and language arts, which are taught entirely in the students' native language. What actually happens in the classroom, however, is usually quite different from what researchers advocate should happen in terms of optimal sequencing and time allotment. By far the greatest difference is that English is the most frequently used language of instruction both within and across the curriculum of most transitional bilingual education programs (Halcon, 1983; Tikunoff, 1983).

There are a number of reasons for why English is favored over the minority language in bilingual classrooms. One major reason is that English proficiency is essential for success in virtually all domains of social interaction outside the home (Hernandez-Chavez, 1984). The fact that English provides access to business, commerce, and the occupational market exerts unrelenting pressure on teachers of LEP students to use English whenever possible, despite programmatic efforts to maintain balanced language use.

A related reason concerns the difficulty many bilingual teachers have in teaching entirely in the non-English language, when English monolinguals and LEP students are grouped together for general instruction. This difficulty seems to be especially prevalent in bilingual programs designed to maintain a strict separation of the two languages on the basis of time or subject matter during the course of the program (Ramirez, 1980; Wong Fillmore, 1982). In the so-called separation approach to bilingual schooling, language distribution over time and within classrooms is a basic curriculum design feature. Consequently, although teachers are supposed to use one language or the other, there is little to prevent them, and much to encourage them to use both concurrently in order to reach the greatest number of students in class. The most common and dreadful form of dual language use in bilingual classrooms is what Saville & Troike (1971) refer to as concurrent translation. In this form of teaching, information presented in one language is repeated or explained in another, presumably so that all students in a bilingual classroom have access to all the material being taught. To be sure, the use of concurrent translation in bilingual classrooms contributes greatly to a language distribution ratio favoring English over the minority language.

In contrast to the separation approach to bilingual instruction, it is also possible to allow for both languages to be used during content instruction, but with clearly expressed guidelines for how switching from one language to another is to occur. In this approach to bilingual instruction, the teacher has to decide on the basis of guidelines when the LEP students' language is appropriate for use as a medium of instruction and when English should serve that purpose.

The most fully developed methodology involving the (non-translation) concurrent use of two languages for bilingual instruction is the New Concurrent Approach (NCA) (Jacobson, 1981a). The NCA incorporates language switching strategies present in the communities served by the school for teaching content and for developing language skills needed to support academic learning. In the NCA classroom, language alternation is structured in terms of four criteria:

1. Both languages are to be used for equal amounts of time;
2. The teaching of content is not to be interrupted;
3. The decision to switch between the two languages is in response to a consciously identified cue;
4. The switch must relate to a specific learning objective (Jacobson, 1983: 120).

Adhering to these criteria requires that language switching behavior in the classroom be controlled in two ways: (1) only inter-sentential switching is allowed, and (2) all language switching is teacher initiated. The meaning of inter-sentential switching within the context of a bilingual classroom is essentially the same as the one associated with community settings: 'a language alternation strategy by which the switching only occurs after one or more sentences have been completed in one language' (Jacobson, 1983: 121).

Studying language distribution in bilingual classrooms

Studies of language use in bilingual classrooms consistently have shown that bilingual teachers use both languages during content instruction, regardless of whether the classroom is organized for separate or concurrent language use (Milk, 1981; Wong Fillmore, 1982). The studies also show that how the two languages are used for instruction differs considerably depending upon how the teacher has been prepared in bilingual methodology (Milk, 1986). Given the apparent ubiquity of dual language use in bilingual classrooms, a logical implication for research is to begin to examine how bilingual teachers make decisions about when and why to use one language or the other for interaction with students during classroom instruction. The rationale for studying bilingual teachers' interactive decision making is straightforward: since any act of teaching is the result of a decision (Shavelson, 1973) and the decision to use one language or the other can affect concept learning as well as language development, learning about interactive decision making can provide useful information concerning the preparation of bilingual teachers.

The purpose of this chapter, therefore, is to introduce a relatively new way of studying language distribution in bilingual classrooms. The proposed methodology draws heavily from research on teachers' thought processes, but especially on teachers' interactive decisions during content instruction. After examining some of the key constructs and models of interactive decision making in general, a model of Bilingual Teacher Interactive Decision Making is presented and described using data from teacher–student interactions in bilingual classrooms. The paper concludes with suggestions for ways to study bilingual teacher interactive decisions.

Interactive decision making

According to Clark & Peterson (1986), on the average, teachers make at least one decision to continue behaving as before or to change behavior approximately every two minutes of interactive teaching. Why so many decisions? One of the earliest answers came from Peterson & Clark (1978). They suggested that all interactive decisions are the result of teachers' judgements concerning how well students are understanding the lesson and whether they are participating appropriately in it. Following Snow's (1972) conceptualization of teacher thinking during classroom instruction, they viewed teaching as a cyclical process in which the teacher observes student behavior, and then makes a judgement of whether the behavior is within acceptable limits, which is followed by a decision to either continue the teaching process unchanged or to initiate an alternative teaching behavior that might bring the student behavior back to a tolerable limit. If no alternatives are available, the teacher continues as previously; however, if a plausible alternative does come to mind, the teacher may decide to engage that alternative by changing the course of instruction, or she might ignore it altogether and continue as before.

Empirical research on teachers' interactive decisions revealed, however, that while teachers did make frequent decisions as predicted, they rarely considered changing their course of action. Moreover, when teachers did give thought to alternatives, they tended to consider no more than two possible strategies from which to choose (Wodlinger, 1980). With these findings in mind, Shavelson & Stern (1981) proposed a new model of interactive decision making based on the assumption that interactive teaching is a matter of carrying out well-established routines. In their model, if student behavior is not within tolerance, the teacher may decide that immediate action is required, and then move to initiate the appropriate routine. However, the teacher may also decide that delayed action is more appropriate than immediate action, or that it is in the best interests of the lesson to continue as before. In any case, the decision made by the teacher is both deliberate and limited to a practiced routine.

In both the Peterson & Clark and Shavelson & Stern models of interactive decision, the observation that student behavior falls outside the range of tolerance is assumed to be the sole antecedent for a decision. It is quite likely, however, that other antecedents come into play. For example, Marland (1977) found that the majority of teachers' reported interactive decisions occurred in response to factors other than deciding that student behavior was not within tolerance. Teachers in the Marland study reported making interactive decisions in response to student questions; when a choice of student to be helped was needed; when a choice of appropriate technique was needed; when there was a transition from one point in the lesson to another; and when the teacher anticipated a problem in comprehension. In other words, Marland found that many of teachers' deliberate decisions to implement a specific action occurred not in response to student behavior, but rather in response to factors originating with the teacher or with the classroom environment itself.

Fogarty, Wang & Creek (1982) also found that cues from sources other than students served as antecedents for a large part of teachers' interactive decisions. This result, coupled with Marland's findings, suggests that any model of teacher interactive decision making should be based upon a definition of interactive decision making as a deliberate choice between continuing to behave a certain way or behaving in a new specific way rather than simply a choice of actions from several possible alternatives. Moreover, the model should reflect the finding that many of teachers' interactive decisions are in response to factors other than judgements about the students' behavior.

Bilingual teacher interactive decision making

In bilingual classrooms organized for separate language use, interactive decisions will be similar to those found in regular, non-bilingual classrooms, since the antecedents of the decision are basically the same. However, as Milk (1981) and Wong Fillmore (1982) have pointed out, many bilingual teachers use two languages for instruction, whether or not there are programmatic efforts to keep them separate. The most common kind of dual language use in bilingual classrooms organized for separate language use is concurrent translation (Swain, 1983). In this case, it appears that a major antecedent for dual language use is the perception that students do not understand the message when that message is not in their native language. For example, when a LEP student does not understand a part of the lesson presented in English, the teacher may routinely decide to implement an alternative course of action; namely, translation into the student's native language, since few other strategies are either available or considered.

Bilingual classrooms following the New Concurrent Approach deliberately use both languages in an alternating fashion for developing important points in a lesson, without translating from one language to the other. NCA teaching involves the use of 16 antecedent cues distributed over four areas to cover the major socio-educational concerns present in a classroom. Table 1 presents the four areas and their corresponding cues. The cues indicate the purpose for switching from one language to another in terms of their relevance to each of the four major areas. For example, within the area of classroom strategies, the teacher may deliberately decide to switch to the other language on the basis of the following needs:

1. for conceptual development in the native language; hence a switch from the second language to the native language;
2. to review a lesson previously taught in the native language; hence, a switch from the native language to the second language.

TABLE 1 *The new concurrent approach cue system*

1. *Classroom strategies*	2. *Curriculum*
a. conceptual reinforcement	a. language appropriateness
b. review	b. topic
c. capturing of attention	c. text
d. praise/reprimand	
3. *Language development*	4. *Interpersonal relationships*
a. variable language dominance	a. intimacy/formality
b. lexical enrichment	b. courtesy
c. translatability	c. free choice
	d. fatigue
	e. self-awareness
	f. rapport

3. to capture attention of students who are distracted; hence a switch to the students' native language.
4. for immediate praise or reprimand; hence a switch to the student's native language (Jacobson, 1981a: 22)

Similar justifications can be made for cues in the remaining three areas.

Teachers learn to respond to the 16 cues by undergoing a carefully planned cue–response training program. In this program the teachers learn to detach themselves from the teaching task and self-monitor their performance in terms of the major pedagogical objectives being pursued. As teachers gain fluency in responding to cues, decisions about which cues to respond to as well as which language to use in the response are expected to become second nature.

Because of the fact that cues have been systematically incorporated into the NCA, and that no other approach to bilingual instruction features anything like them, the NCA offers an interesting context for studying teachers' interactive decision making. Not only does the NCA reflect the idea that teachers respond to cues other than student behavior, but also to the notion that a decision must be based on a deliberate choice to implement a specific action. A model of bilingual teacher interactive decision making is shown in Figure 1. This model is partially based upon the work of Shavelson & Stern (1981). In particular, it is modified to incorporate the idea of multiple antecedents to interactive decisions, and that teachers tend to rely upon well-established routines as they move through a lesson.

The model allows for five possible decision paths. In the first path, the teacher observes a cue that signals a possible change in behavior, but decides that the cue is within tolerance, and continues the routine. In the second path, the teacher observes a cue that signals a possible change in behavior, and decides to implement a specific action as well as to switch to the other language. In the third path, the teacher decides to implement a specific action, but does not switch to the other language. The decision not to switch means that too little time has been spent in the language currently in use. Maintaining a balanced distribution of the two languages without engaging in intra-sentential language switching and excessive alternation is an essential goal of NCA methodology (Milk, 1986).

In the fourth path, the teacher observes a cue signaling a possible change in behavior, and decides to delay any specific action, while keeping in mind the amount of time spent in that language. Again, keeping track of time is necessary to counteract the pull exerted by English, the dominant language, and to preserve a balanced use of the two languages. In the fifth

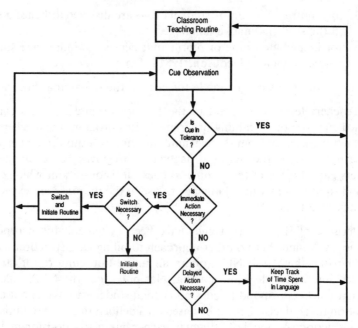

FIGURE 1   *A model of bilingual teacher interactive decision making*

path, the teacher observes a cue, decides that it is not within tolerance, but decides neither to implement a new routine nor to delay action. In this case, the teacher also chooses to ignore the amount of time spent in the language. Of the five paths, only the fifth one would be considered undesirable, since not only is the teacher not keeping track of the time factor, but is ignoring the need for possibly behaving in a more effective way as well.

The purpose of presenting the Bilingual Teacher Interactive Decision Model is to offer an analytical framework to begin studying how bilingual teachers who use two languages during content instruction make decisions about when to use which language and what triggers that decision. The model can be useful for designing research to describe the teaching process from the point of view of interactive decision making rather than from a strict behavioral perspective found in most studies conducted in bilingual classrooms (see Long, 1983 for a review of language classroom research methodology).

For example, Table 2 presents a sample lesson by a teacher trained in NCA methodology (Jacobson, 1981b). In this lesson the justifications for implementing new routines and for switching languages are presented. The

TABLE 2 *A language switching dialogue using the NCA cue system*

T: Do you remember what we have been learning about air?
Robert, what have we learned about air and weight?

S1: ...that air has weight.

T: Very good. Isela, what have we learned about air and space?

S2: ...that air takes up space.

T: Very good.

REVIEW (1b)

T: ¿Se acuerdan del experimento que hicimos el otro día con el vaso y la toallita de papel?

T: Lorenzo, ¿me puedes decir lo que hicimos?

S3: Pusimos una toallita en un vaso y no se mojó el papel.

T: Muy bien, Lorenzo.

CONCEPTUAL REINFORCEMENT (1a)

T: Who can tell me now why the paper didn't get wet?

S4: ...because the air in the cup didn't let the water in.

PRAISE (1d)

T: Muy bien, Laura, tu sí pusiste atención. El papel no se mojó porque el aire ocupa espacio o lugar en el vaso y no permite que entre el agua.

TEXT (2c)

T: Now, I want you to turn to page 18—a one and an eight—Here you will see another experiment.

T: Isela, en el experimento este, ¿qué ves tu que está haciendo el niño?

(Continued)

TABLE 2 *Continued*

S2: Le está echando aqua a un vaso y le está poniendo un papel arriba.

T: Muy bien.

TEXT (2c)

T: Let's now read on page 18 to see why he's pouring water in a glass and putting a paper on top. (The teacher reads and elaborates in English.)

CONCEPTUAL REINFORCEMENT (1a)

T: Entonces podemos decir que el niño quiere comprobar que el aire empuja por todos los lados, ¿verdad? Raul, entonces el niño quiere comprobar que el aire empuja por todos los lados ¿haciendo qué?

S1: el experimento.

T: Muy bien.

VARIABLE LANGUAGE DOMINANCE (3a)

T: The little boy is doing an experiment and we are going to prove too that air pushes from all sides, but first I want to show you something.

CAPTURING OF ATTENTION (1c)

T: Carmen, ¿me puedes decir si si esta ilustración del vaso y el papel se parecen al vaso y el papel en el libro?

S5: Si.

Bilingual Teacher Interactive Decision Model predicts that the teacher will follow one or more of the five paths presented above. As can be seen, this bilingual teacher stays primarily within the second path. However, additional information is needed to learn the kinds of decisions that the teacher was really making as she progressed through the lesson. There are several questions that could be raised about this sample: what kinds of cues do NCA bilingual teachers report using?; which cues are used more frequently?; would the teacher in this sample provide the same reasons for switching that Jacobson does? The reason that answers to these kinds of descriptive questions are important is because at some point, researchers will need to identify the kinds of interactive decisions effective bilingual teachers make so that this information can be used to increase bilingual teachers' effectiveness in general.

Now that the Bilingual Teacher Interaction Decision Model has been presented along with an example to illustrate its use, the final step in this paper is to consider how to study bilingual teachers' interactive decisions as they occur during actual classroom interaction. The most promising research method is the Stimulated Recall Technique (Clark & Peterson, 1981).

The goal of stimulated recall is to elicit self-reports of teachers' interactive thoughts and decisions. The procedure is relatively simple: The teacher is video recorded during content instruction for at least one full lesson, and then asked to view the video tape as a means to stimulate recall of interactive decisions during the lessons. The teacher can be allowed to select videotaped segments to be the focus of the interview, or both the interviewer and the teacher can jointly select the segments. A third possibility is for the interviewer to decide which segments of the videotape will be the focus of the interview.

The interview itself can be either of a clinical nature where the interviewer using probe questions encourages the teacher to describe what is happening and why; or it can be highly structured, relying on a set of predetermined questions (see Clark & Peterson, 1986: 270–271).

Here is an example of the kinds of questions used in a structured interview with a teacher upon seeing a taped segment of teaching:

1. What were you doing in this segment and why?
2. Were you thinking of alternative actions or strategies of teaching at that time?
3. What were you noticing about the students as you made your decision?

4. Did any student reactions cause you to act differently than you had planned?
5. Do you remember any aspects of the situation that might have affected what you did in this segment (Clark & Peterson, 1986: 268)?

Teachers' responses to the interview are audiotaped so they can be coded into specific categories and then tallied.

The stimulated recall technique could be easily adapted for bilingual instruction where the teacher makes language distribution decisions on the basis of a system of cues, such as the one presented in Table 1 above. This technique enables researchers to know more about what triggers language switching in bilingual classrooms, and which kinds of switches promote language development and content understanding. More to the point, it suggests a new way to study effective bilingual instruction by focusing on teachers' decision making during that highly complex and cognitively demanding process known as teaching. The study of bilingual interactive decision making, then, is a new research challenge for bilingual education.

References

CLARK, C. and PETERSON, P. 1981, Stimulated-recall. In B.R. JOYCE, C.C. BROWN and L. PECK (eds), *Flexibility in Teaching: An Excursion into the Nature of Teaching and Training*. New York: Longman.
—— 1986, Teachers' thought processes. In M. WITTROCK (ed.), *Handbook of Research on Teaching: Third Edition* (pp. 255–296). New York: Macmillan Publishing Company.
CUMMINS, J. 1981, The role of primary language development in promoting educational success for language minority students. In *Schooling and Language Minority Students: A Theoretical Framework* (pp. 3–49). Los Angeles: Evaluation and Dissemination and Assessment Center.
FOGARTY, J., WANG, M. and CREEK, R. 1982, A descriptive study of experiences and novice teachers; interactive instructional decision processes. Paper presented at the Annual Meeting of the American Educational Research Association, New York City.
General Accounting Office 1987, Bilingual education: A new look at the research evidence. Briefing Report to the Chairman, Committee on Education and Labor, House of Representatives. GAO/DEM-87-12R, Washington DC.
HALCON, J.J. 1983, A structural profile of basic Title VII (Spanish–English) bilingual bicultural education programs. *NABE Journal* 7(3), 55–73.
HERNANDEZ-CHAVEZ, E. 1984, The inadequacy of English immersion education as an educational approach for language minority students in the United States. In *Studies in Immersion Education: Collection for United States Educators* (pp. 144–183). Sacramento: California State Department of Education.
JACOBSON, R. 1981a, The implementation of a bilingual instructional model: The

new concurrent approach. In R. PADILLA (ed.), *Ethnoperspectives in Bilingual Education Research. Vol. III: Bilingual Education Technology* (pp. 14–29). Ypsilanti, MI: Eastern Michigan University.

—— 1981b, A demonstration project in bilingual methodology. Unpublished Manuscript, University of Texas at San Antonio.

—— 1983, Can two languages be developed concurrently? Recent developments in bilingual methodology. In H. ALTMAN and M. MCCLURE (eds), *Dimension: Language '82* (pp. 110–131). Louisville, KY: University of Louisville.

LEGARRETA, D. 1979, The effects of program models on language acquisition by Spanish-speaking children. *TESOL Quarterly* 13(4), 9–16.

LONG, M. 1983, Inside the 'black box': Methodological issues in classroom research on language learning. In H.W. SELIGER and M.H. LONG (eds), *Classroom Oriented Research in Second Language Acquisition* (pp. 3–35). Rowley, MA: Newbury House.

MARLAND, R. 1977, A study of teachers' interactive thoughts. Unpublished Doctoral Dissertation, University of Alberta, Edmonton, Canada.

MILK, R. 1981, An analysis of the functional allocation of Spanish and English in a bilingual classroom. *CABE Research Journal* 2(2), 11–26.

—— 1986, The issue of language separation in bilingual methodology. In E. GARCIA and B. FLORES (eds), *Language and Literacy Research in Bilingual Education* (pp. 67–86). Tempe, AZ: Arizona State University.

PETERSON, P. and CLARK, C. 1978, Teacher planning, teacher behavior, and student achievement. *American Educational Research Journal* 15, 417–432.

RAMIREZ, A. 1980, Language in bilingual classrooms. *NABE Journal* 4(3), 61–79.

SAVILLE, M. and TROIKE, R. 1971, *Handbook of Bilingual Education.* Washington, DC: Teachers of English to Speakers of Other Languages.

SHAVELSON, R. 1973, The basic teaching skill: Decision making. R & D Memorandum No. 104, Stanford University, School of Education, Center for R & D in Teaching.

SHAVELSON, R. and STERN, P. 1981, Research on teacher's pedagogical thoughts, judgements, decisions, and behavior. *Review of Educational Research* 3, 455–98.

SNOW, R. 1972, A model teacher training system: An overview. R & D Memorandum No. 92, Stanford University, School of Education, Center for R & D in Teaching. (ERIC Document Reproduction Service No. ED 066 437.)

SWAIN, M. 1983, Bilingualism without tears. In M. CLARKE and J. HANDSCOMBE (eds), *On Tesol '82: Pacific Perspectives on Language Learning and Teaching* (pp. 35–48). Washington, DC: Teachers of English to Speakers of Other Languages.

TIKUNOFF, W. 1983, *An Emerging Description of Successful Bilingual Instruction: An Executive Summary of Part 1 of the SBIF Descriptive Study.* San Francisco: Far West Laboratory.

WODLINGER, M. 1980, A study of teacher interactive decision making. Unpublished Doctoral Dissertation, University of Alberta, Edmonton, Canada.

WONG FILLMORE, L. 1982, Instructional language as linguistic input: Second language learning in classrooms. In L.C. WILKINSON (ed.), *Communicating in the Classroom* (pp. 283–296). New York: Academic Press.

WONG FILLMORE, L. and VALADEZ, C. 1986, Teaching bilingual learners. In M. WITTROCK (ed.), *Handbook of Research on Teaching: Third Edition* (pp. 648–685). New York: Macmillan Publishing Company.

Section II
Interactional Considerations

5 Classroom talk in English immersion, early-exit and late-exit transitional bilingual education programs

J. DAVID RAMIREZ and BARBARA J. MERINO

Introduction

The number of limited-English-proficient (LEP) students in the United States is increasing (Waggoner, 1981). This increase has led researchers to focus on the need to identify instructional programs that effectively meet the special learning needs of LEP students. To answer the question of relative effectiveness, it is necessary to first define the instructional model, identifying those classroom processes deemed important to student learning and understand the inter-relationships of these processes. To date little is known about how the instructional programs provided to LEP students function within the classroom. As a result, even less is known about the relative effectiveness of specific classroom practices with respect to learning of LEP students.

Studies to date which have conducted direct classroom observation of LEP students have sampled a limited number of classrooms, ranging from an N of 1 (Schultz, 1975) to 58 (Tikunoff & Vazquez-Faria, 1982). Moreover, these studies were also limited in the range of grade levels and/or program models examined. Frequently only one grade level was considered (Legarreta, 1977, 1979) and/or program model variation was not taken into account (Tikunoff & Vazquez-Faria, 1982). The one study that did address the instructional process in elementary classrooms across grades and program models (Wong Fillmore et al., 1985) did so by using essentially a rating procedure and ethnographic techniques rather than time-line coding to describe classroom process.

The study we report on here is based on observations of 103 classrooms. Data were collected from first and second grade classrooms from three different instructional program models implemented in seven school districts from widely different areas in the United States (California, Texas, Florida, New Jersey and New York). The three program models were English immersion, early-exit and late-exit transitional bilingual education programs. The focus of this study was to specifically identify those instructional processes considered to be important for second language learning, examine their inter-relationships, and determine if there were teaching styles unique to each instructional model. These instructional styles could then be compared with respect to their relative effectiveness in meeting the learning needs of LEP students. As the data for this study are part of an ongoing longitudinal study, child outcome data were defined for now in terms of the frequency with which LEP students initiated conversations with teachers and produced language in the classroom. These variables were selected on the assumption that among the necessary conditions for second language learning is the opportunity to produce the target language (Swain, 1984) and negotiate with it (Long, 1981).

The principal purpose of this study is to investigate the nature of program implementation in the three program models, structured English immersion, early-exit, and late-exit transition bilingual programs. This study addressed the following questions: What language use patterns were exhibited in the three program models? Do the three programs under study in fact represent three distinct instructional programs? And if they do represent three different programs, do they represent the three programs of interest in this study—immersion strategy, early-exit, and late-exit transitional bilingual education programs? Finally, do teachers differ in their effectiveness in maximizing student output?

What instructional programs are provided to language-minority children?

We turn now to a more complete discussion of the program models. Four alternative instructional programs have evolved to serve language-minority children in the United States: (a) submersion, (b) English as a second language (ESL), (c) transitional bilingual education (TBE), and (d) structured English immersion strategy (SEIS). These programs differ in five main areas: (a) whether traditional all-English instruction is used, (b) whether special instruction in English as a subject is provided, (c) whether

English is taught through the teaching of other subjects, (d) whether non-language subjects such as mathematics are taught in the primary language of the limited-English-proficient students, and (e) whether the primary language of limited-English-proficient students is used (to supplement instruction in English). The following describes the four programs in terms of these characteristics.

The *submersion* approach is typical of the services provided to the majority of language-minority students (Office of Bilingual Bicultural Education, 1981). In submersion programs, language-minority children are placed in ordinary mainstream classrooms where only English is spoken. No special provisions are made in these mainstream classrooms to help these students learn the English skills they need to succeed in school. Students may or may not receive English as a second language instruction (ESL).

In typical *ESL* programs, language-minority students spend most of their day in a submersion classroom, but do receive some extra instruction in English. This special instruction is specifically developed to teach English as a second language. For subjects other than English, the language-minority students study the school's standard curriculum in English-only classrooms. In teaching ESL, the teacher may or may not use the primary language of the limited-English-proficient students.

In *TBE* programs, language-minority students study subject *matter* in their primary language until they have learned enough English to succeed in English-only mainstream classrooms. Children in TBE programs should learn to read first in their non-English home language and then in English. ESL is often used as a supplement to reduce the time needed to learn English. TBE programs are similar to submersion and ESL in that English is usually taught as a separate subject, but differ in that other content areas, including reading, are taught in the child's non-English home language, at least in principle.

In very general terms, transitional bilingual education programs fall into one of two instructional models—early-exit and late-exit. While they are similar in many ways, they differ substantially in the role of L1 and the length of treatment. In an early-exit program, the development of L1 is not a goal. This is reflected in the limited way L1 is developed and used for content area instruction. Generally, L1 is used for approximately one hour per day in kindergarten and quickly tapers off in grades one and two. Moreover, L1 is used not so much to teach the content areas as it is used to clarify and support instruction provided in English. Students are mainstreamed into English-only programs as soon as they demonstrate proficiency in English, usually occurring within two or three years after entry into the program. Thus, a LEP student entering kindergarten would be mainstreamed at the end of first or second grade. In contrast, L1 development is a goal in late-exit programs evident in the efforts taken to develop L1 proficiency and the extensive use of L1 for content area instruction (approximately 50% of total instructional time). Moreover, a student is not mainstreamed until after the fifth or sixth grade, regardless of when English proficiency is demonstrated.

The *SEIS* program is proposed by some educators and policy makers as an alternative to ESL and TBE programs (Bakers & DeKanter, 1981; Peña-Hughes, 1982). It is based on the results of Canadian French immersion programs for language majority (i.e. English) speakers (Ramirez *et al.*, 1986). While similar to ESL and some TBE programs in many ways, the SEIS also differs from them substantially. All instruction is in English. Rather than teaching English strictly as a subject, however, the SEIS endeavors to teach English through the various content areas. Prior knowledge of English is not assumed. Instead, teachers in SEISs carefully tailor their English to a level that limited-English-proficient students can understand. Such teaching differs from transitional bilingual programs in that SEISs present the subject matter exclusively in English, while TBE programs teach content in the students' primary language while they are learning English.

The SEIS teacher is bilingual and speaks the students' non-English home language. The students may use their primary language among themselves and to address the teacher. Generally, however, the teacher speaks to the students in English, using the home language only occasionally to provide or clarify instructions. Because of the limited use of L1 and because of the dramatically different social context in which the United States and Canadian models operate, many educators in the United States have questioned the viability of this model for the education of language minority students in the United States (Hernandez-Chavez, 1984).

While these program definitions very broadly outline the framework in which these programs operate, they do little to concretely operationalize how languages are actually used inside the classroom. In fact, there is wide consensus among practitioners and researchers of bilingual education in the United States, that in practice these programs are best defined administratively in fiscal terms, as programs which receive a certain type of funding, because many in fact, seldom if ever use the primary language of the children they serve (Wong Fillmore *et al.*, 1983). Moreover, even within bilingual programs that actually use two languages the distribution patterns may vary a great deal (Legarreta, 1977). Nonetheless, this consensus stems more from anecdotal observations or limited data rather than from large scale studies of bilingual classrooms.

How is language used in the classroom for instruction? What are effective teaching behaviors in second language programs?

We turn now to a brief discussion of previous research on language use patterns and effective teaching behaviors in second language programs. Here we are concerned with two principal questions: How has research on classroom process been conducted? and, what insights on effective classroom practices does this research offer? In searching for effective program models for teaching language-minority children, recent research has turned away from simple comparisons of students' achievement under different treatments. This shift has come from a rediscovery of a truism in educational research that before program effects can be analyzed, the program treatment must be defined operationally and observed systematically to insure that it is in place (Baker & DeKanter, 1981; Willig, 1985; Wong Fillmore & Valadez, 1986). To date very few studies on bilingual education actually include observational data of program implementation in the classroom. Of those studies that have, four approaches have been used in effecting observational studies of language use in bilingual classrooms. Borrowing from the research paradigms of the teacher effectiveness literature (Dunkin & Biddle, 1974; Long, 1983), researchers have described (1) the process in which the two languages are used with bilingual children (Shultz, 1975; Milk, 1980); (2) the relationship of process to context, for example, the distribution of language use in different program models (Legarreta, 1977); (3) the relationship of process to process, for example, how the use of certain behaviors by teachers, such as feedback, can affect the responses of students (Chaudron, 1977); and (4) the relationship of process to product, in which effective teaching behaviors are identified in relationship to language use and their effect in promoting student achievement (Ramirez & Stromquist, 1979; Legarreta, 1979).

Process studies

Much of the early observational work of bilingual classrooms used a case study approach in which language use was simply described in one classroom or program. Thus Mackey (1972) described language use patterns in the John F. Kennedy School in Berlin. Schultz (1975), studying a bilingual classroom in Boston, found that teachers tended to favor the use of English, using Spanish principally to control behavior. Students and teachers perceived that it was better not to use Spanish. Schultz found that most complex academic instruction was conducted in English. His approach relied on ethnographic techniques to describe the nature of classroom discourse (Trueba & Wright, 1981). This type of research is particularly effective in identifying further lines of inquiry for later more controlled studies. The principal limitation of this approach however, is in establishing a link to effectiveness and in the use of these techniques with large numbers of classrooms.

Process/context studies

The distribution of language use in relationship to the program model was first studied systematically by Legarreta (1977), who observed bilingual kindergarten classrooms in California in the early 1970s using real time coding and a category observation instrument. With a category system, each event is coded each time that it occurs. She found that teachers using a concurrent translation model often favored English, with many of them speaking English 80% of the time. However, when the languages were separated by day, with instruction provided in one language one day and in the other the next, the so-called alternate day model, the language use distribution was more nearly equal. In some studies the analysis of the type of language used in different program models has focused on the use of specific structures. Thus Hamayan & Tucker (1980), also using a category system, observed through audio recordings three teachers from two immersion schools and three teachers from two French schools in Montreal. They tallied the frequency of occurrence of nine grammatical structures and found no difference in the speech samples from each classroom. They also reported no differences between immersion and non-immersion classrooms in the general teaching strategies used. That is, teachers in both program models tended to manipulate questioning, reinforcement and error correction in similar ways, further suggesting that teacher classroom discourse, at least when analyzed broadly, tended to be similar across these program models. The principal strengths of these studies are that they used observation procedures with high reliability and analyzed differences across program models. Their principal weakness is that they observed such few classrooms of each program model that it is difficult to discriminate between teacher and program differences.

Process/product

Typically, researchers of classroom process have focused on the relationship of teachers' and students' behaviors to an outcome. Usually the outcome or product has been student achievement. Thus Ramirez & Stromquist (1979; Politzer, 1977) videotaped 18 bilingual elementary classroom teachers teaching English as a second language and attempted to relate student gains to specific teacher behaviors. Included among the behaviors that were strongly related to student gains in production were: (1) requiring students to manipulate concrete objects following a teacher command, (2) questioning students regarding information previously presented by the teacher, (3) explaining the meaning of new words, (4) correcting students' grammatical errors directly by providing the correct structure, and (5) varying the type of teacher behaviors. Modeling and correction of pronunciation errors were negatively related to student gains. The advantage of this type of study is that it directly relates specific instructional practices to student gains. However, this kind of study only looks at classroom behavior and neglects individual differences in the learner, such as motivation and cognitive style and their interaction with the learning process. Moreover, these studies are correlational. Thus particular behaviors cannot be said to cause student gains but to simply co-occur with them.

Another approach used to observe classrooms relies on the use of a rating scale where the frequency of an event is recorded on a continuum from low to high. Wong Fillmore and her associates (1985) used such an approach in their analyses of 17 bilingual and English-only classrooms. Using a combination of audio, video and live recording, third and fifth grade classrooms were observed over a one year period. Successful and unsuccessful classrooms were identified on the basis of student gains made on oral language and achievement tests. Variables that were related to gains in production skills in English included: interactional opportunities (e.g. fair allocation of turns), quality of instructional language (e.g. contextualization of information), and quality of teaching (e.g. clarity of instructional goals). The effect of these variables affected Chinese and Hispanic students differentially at times, particularly with gains made in comprehension. Thus interactional opportunities, or contact with peers, appeared to be beneficial to Hispanics but not to Chinese students. The principal strength of such a rating approach is that it permits observation of high inference and more complex behaviors. Its principal drawbacks are its subjectivity and fallibility across observers and observations. Another problem with this study is the lack of a clear definition and adherence to a program model. The classrooms observed by Wong Fillmore, for example, revealed an average usage of L1 of 8% and a range of 0–24%. It's difficult to establish effective bilingual classroom techniques when the program model is so little adhered to.

Process/process

In another tradition, researchers have investigated the nature of teachers' and students' language use patterns in the classroom and how they may affect each other. Thus Gaies (1977) and Chaudron (1979) found that teachers adjust the complexity of their speech to ESL students on the basis of the students' proficiency. Holley & King (1971, cited in Cohen, 1975) reported that increasing the amount of wait time when asking second language students a question increased the number of correct responses. Schinke-Llano (1983) found that some teachers in elementary bilingual classrooms in Illinois treat fluent and limited-English-proficient students differentially, addressing fewer academically oriented utterances to the limited-English speakers, for example. Other studies have focused on the relationship of teacher strategies in second language classrooms to student engagement (Nerenz & Knop, 1983; Tikunoff & Vazques-Faria, 1982) or to student perceptions of effectiveness (Omaggio, 1982). The fundamental importance of these types of studies is that they strive to understand the process of teaching as it proceeds rather than focusing on the product at the end of the process. Their principal weakness is that they can only identify how they relate to other classroom behaviors and not to achievement.

The approach used to observe in this study focused on testing out several hypotheses about effective teaching for language minority students. Based on a review of the literature, an earlier more complex system used audiotaped data (Ramirez *et al.*, 1986; Chaudron, 1985). However, as the number of classrooms increased from 86 to over 172, it was necessary to develop a live coding system to observe teacher/student interaction in the classroom (Ramirez, Merino & Yuen, 1985).

Methodology

Sample selection

Four steps were followed to identify study sites. In step 1, we conducted a national telephone survey of state educational agencies, bilingual educators, members of bilingual program support agencies, educational administrators, and organizations to identify potential programs. Those interviewed were asked if they knew of elementary instructional programs serving limited-English-proficient students which matched the program descriptions presented earlier in this paper. In step 2 staff were contacted from each referred program by telephone to verify the extent to which our selection criteria (i.e. program descriptions) were met. Step 3 required a visit by study staff to the most promising sites to confirm program characteristics. Finally, step 4 consisted of a letter of invitation to those programs that most closely resembled the program models described in this study. This resulted in the selection and participation of five immersion strategy sites and three late-exit transitional programs. Four early-exit transitional bilingual education sites were selected from four of the districts implementing an immersion strategy program. The fifth early-exit program was selected in a school district adjacent to the fifth immersion strategy program site which did not offer an early-exit program.

Instrumentation

The Language Observation Measure (LOM) documents how teachers and students use language in the classroom. The purpose of the LOM is to enable observers to accurately document language use in the classroom. The LOM is structured to describe the communication between teachers and students. The unit of analysis is time based. That is, on the minute, the observer looks up and following explicit rules, first identifies the beginning of an exchange. Secondly, the observer then codes certain language behaviors within a specific category system. The language behaviors are referred to in this discussion as utterances. An utterance is a speaker's turn in a turn-taking sequence (i.e. communicative exchange). This time sampling approach of teacher language has been used in teacher effectiveness studies (Program on Teaching Effectiveness—Stanford University, 1976) and in bilingual classrooms (Legarreta, 1977). The observer codes a number of characteristics about the teacher–student interaction: [The observer codes] who initiated the exchange, the language used, and the specific language behavior used to start the exchange. Then the respondent is identified, as is the language used and the specific responding language behavior. In those instances where the initiator of the exchange reacts to the response, the specific follow-up language behavior is coded along with the specific language used. The exchange is described further by documentation of the following for each exchange:

Function. The purpose or overall intent of each turn in the exchange.
Focus. Whether each turn in the exchange is concerned with how things are said (form) vs. with what is said (concept).
Activity. The sanctioned classroom activity providing the context for the exchange.
Realia. Whether visuals, objects, and/or physical gestures are used to support the language behaviors exhibited.

Content. The subject area that is being taught at the time the observation is made.

These last behaviors provide the contextual framework for understanding the specific language behaviors noted for each exchange, turn-taking sequence.

Each classroom was observed twice for approximately three hours each, once in the morning and once in the afternoon. In general, two weeks separated the two observations. With the exception of physical education classes, lunch, and recess, the observations represent the daily instructional program provided to the limited-English proficient students participating in this study.

At each observation, the observers observed and coded classroom language consecutively for 10 minutes. At each minute, the observer would look up and code the first complete teacher–student exchange. If after one minute no exchange was observed (e.g. students are taking a test and teacher is monitoring) the observer nonetheless coded teacher and student behavior at that moment. Thus the observer would code 10 teacher–student interactions (or the absence of such) in 10 minutes. Four 10 minute observations were done per hour. Observers were trained over a two week period through the use of video tapes and live practice observations. All observers exceeded the 85% reliability standard required for observations.

There is substantial evidence documenting how the physical and social context of the environment affects human behavior (Moos, 1976). With this understanding data were collected which describe the context of teacher–student exchanges. They include: classroom activities, content areas, and measures of student task engagement.

Across what classroom activities were observations made?

Whenever an exchange was recorded between the teacher and student(s), the type of classroom activity in which the exchange was taking place was coded. Classroom activities were coded into one of eight categories: (a) presentation (students are listening to a presentation of material or directions from the teacher); (b) discussion (students are talking about appropriate content area); (c) seatwork (students are engaged in seatwork such as workbook, writing, silent reading, or other sanctioned non-academic activities such as puzzles, etc.); (d) drillwork (students are engaged in oral repetition); (e) listening (students are attending to audio equipment such as tape recorder, radio, or phonograph); (f) interim (students are waiting for teacher's attention, sharpening a pencil, or lining up for recess); (g) reading (students are reading aloud); and (h) other (students are engaged in activities other than those described above, e.g. watching a filmstrip, working at the chalkboard, doing a science experiment, not fooling around).

Consistently across programs and grades, discussion is one of the major classroom activities, followed by seatwork. Nonetheless, some program differences by grade level are noted. Late-exit first graders were provided with more interim activity (25.6%) than were immersion strategy students (15.2%) or early-exit students (13.6%) (see Table 1). No other striking program or grade level differences are noteworthy.

TABLE 1 *Mean proportion of classroom activities by program and grade*

		Program		
Grade		Immersion strategy	Early- exit	Late- exit
	Mean frequency	$\bar{X} = 175.3$	$\bar{X} = 172.0$	$\bar{X} = 163.7$
1	% Presentation	4.9	3.6	3.9
	% Discussion	39.0	41.9	34.5
	% Seatwork	27.9	26.5	28.2
	% Drill	4.7	4.6	1.3
	% Listening	1.1	2.3	1.1
	% Interim	15.2	13.6	25.6
	% Reading	5.8	5.1	5.3
	% Other	1.3	2.4	0.0
	Mean frequency	$\bar{X} = 173.8$	$\bar{X} = 183.8$	$\bar{X} = 170.5$
2	% Presentation	6.5	6.4	4.5
	% Discussion	36.4	37.9	44.1
	% Seatwork	31.3	27.7	32.8
	% Drill	5.1	2.3	2.8
	% Listening	1.2	3.2	0.9
	% Interim	13.8	9.0	8.6
	% Reading	4.4	10.4	4.0
	% Other	0.8	3.1	2.3

Across what content areas were observations made?

Whenever an exchange between a teacher and student was recorded, content area was coded into one of seven areas: (a) reading, (b) language arts, (c) math, (d) social studies, (e) non-academic (e.g. art, music), (f) other academic (e.g. science, computer science), and (g) procedures (e.g. lining up for recess, collecting lunch money, taking attendance). Observations were made across all these areas in each program and grade. Nonetheless, program differences by grade are noted. Most of the differences in first grade occur in reading, other academic and procedures. Immersion and early-exit first grade students were observed more often during reading (28.0% and 27.8%, respectively) than were late-exit students (13.0%) (see Table 2). However, late-exit students were observed more often during other academic (15.8%) and procedures (23.9%) than were

TABLE 2 *Mean proportion of observations by content area, program, and grade*

		Program		
		Immersion strategy	*Early-exit*	*Late-exit*
Grade				
	Mean frequency	$\bar{X} = 175.3$	$\bar{X} = 172.0$	$\bar{X} = 163.7$
1	% Reading	28.0	27.8	13.0
	% Language arts	28.5	24.7	23.1
	% Math	13.8	18.0	18.4
	% Social studies	6.0	6.8	3.9
	% Non-academic	6.0	7.9	2.0
	% Other academic	3.7	2.1	15.8
	% Procedures	14.0	12.7	23.9
	Mean frequency	$\bar{X} = 173.8$	$\bar{X} = 183.8$	$\bar{X} = 170.5$
2	% Reading	22.9	28.9	15.3
	% Language arts	29.6	26.0	39.1
	% Math	16.8	19.3	19.2
	% Social studies	3.2	4.9	4.6
	% Non-academic	6.0	4.2	2.7
	% Other academic	8.9	8.9	8.8
	% Procedures	12.5	7.7	10.2

either immersion (3.7% and 14.0%, respectively) or early-exit students (2.1% and 12.7%, respectively).

A few program differences were also noted in the second grade. As in first grade, immersion and early-exit students were observed more during reading (22.9% and 28.9%, respectively) periods than were late-exit students (15.3%). In contrast to first grade, late-exit students were observed more often during language arts (39.1%) than were either immersion (29.6%) or early-exit (26.0%) students.

Does students' task engagement vary by program or grade?

No. Data consistently show that students across programs and grades are engaged in their assigned tasks the majority of the time that they were observed (i.e. 83.3%–90.1%).

Do student grouping patterns vary by program and grade?

Somewhat. Teachers across programs and grades tend to cluster students in large groups (> 10 students), rather than in medium (6–10 students), small (2–5 students), or in individual (1 student) groups. Late-exit teachers use large groups more often in first grade (70.6%) than do first grade immersion strategy teachers (51.3%) or early-exit (46.3%) teachers. However, second grade immersion strategy (50.9%) and early-exit (51.4%) teachers use large groups slightly more often than do late-exit teachers (42.5%).

Results

Which language is used?

As defined in this study, immersion strategy, early-exit, and late-exit transitional bilingual programs are differentiated primarily on the basis of the language(s) used in the classroom and the amount each is used. All formal instruction in immersion strategy classrooms should be in English, with little or no use of Spanish. Both English and Spanish are used for instruction in early-exit and late-exit classrooms. However, Spanish is used at least 40% of the time through grade 6 in late-exit classrooms. In contrast, teachers in early-exit programs dramatically taper the use of Spanish for instruction after kindergarten.

Does the language use pattern observed in the study's programs match the patterns described above?

Yes. Tables 3 and 4 show dramatic differences in the proportion of English used between the three programs ($F = 57.14$, df $= 2$, $p = 0.0001$) and grades within programs ($F = 3.98$, df $= 1$, $p = 0.04$). However, only significant program differences were noted in the use of Spanish ($F = 59.97$, df $= 2$, $p = 0.0001$). For example, first grade teachers in the immersion strategy program almost always use English (97.5%) and rarely use Spanish (1.2%) (see Table 3). Early-exit first grade teachers use English two-thirds of the time (67.7%) and Spanish about one-third of the time (30.6%). In marked contrast, first grade teachers in late-exit programs use English less than one-fourth (22.1%) of the time and use Spanish slightly more than three-fourths (76.8%). Second grade teachers display a similar pattern across programs. However, when all non-verbal behaviors are considered (i.e. non-verbal, no response, and listening), the proportion of non-verbal behaviors seems to be fairly constant across program models and grades (10.7% to 14.0%).

Does the student's use of English or Spanish differ between programs?

Yes. Student language use patterns are very similar to those of their teachers. First grade children in immersion strategy programs almost always use English (97.6%) and infrequently use Spanish (2.3%). In early-exit programs, first grade children use English two-thirds (62.7%) and Spanish about one-third (36.0%) of the time. Noticeably different, late-exit first grade students tend not to use much English (21.0%) and to use mostly Spanish (78.2%). Immersion strategy second graders use mostly English (96.5%) and rarely use Spanish (3.1%). Second grade early-exit students use slightly more English (71.6%) and less Spanish (27.2%) than that of their first grade counterparts.

To what degree are students given opportunities to use language?

When the frequency of student (see Table 4) and teacher (see Table 3) behaviors are compared, clearly, teachers do most of the talking, producing from two to three times as many utterances as do students. Typically, over three-fourths (75.4% to 78.4%) of student interactions with teachers are responses to teacher initiations (see Table 14). Moreover, approximately half (45.2% to 58.9%) of all student interactions with teachers are non-verbal (see Table 5).

TABLE 3 *Mean* proportion of teacher verbal behaviors by language, program and grade*

Grade		Program		
		Immersion strategy	Early-exit	Late-exit
	Mean frequency	$\bar{X} = 208.4$	$\bar{X} = 191.1$	$\bar{X} = 168.3$
1	% English	97.5	67.7	22.1
	% Spanish	1.2	30.6	76.8
	% Mixed	1.3	1.6	1.2
	Mean frequency	$\bar{X} = 199.1$	$\bar{X} = 213.6$	$\bar{X} = 211.7$
2	% English	98.3	75.0	40.7
	% Spanish	1.4	23.1	58.0
	% Mixed	0.3	1.8	1.3

* Mean teacher utterance is defined as the average number of utterances made by teachers during the period of observation, approximately five hours.

TABLE 4 *Mean proportion of student verbal behaviors by language, program and grade*

Grade		Program		
		Immersion strategy	Early-exit	Late-exit
	Mean frequency	$\bar{X} = 96.6$	$\bar{X} = 94.3$	$\bar{X} = 68.5$
1	% English	97.6	62.7	21.0
	% Spanish	2.3	36.0	78.2
	% Mixed	0.1	1.4	0.8
	Mean frequency	$\bar{X} = 95.9$	$\bar{X} = 94.3$	$\bar{X} = 99.6$
2	% English	96.5	71.6	41.3
	% Spanish	3.1	27.2	54.8
	% Mixed	0.3	1.2	3.9

TABLE 5 *Mean proportion of student verbal and non-verbal behaviors by language, program and grade*

		Program		
Grade		Immersion strategy	Early-exit	Late-exit
	Mean frequency	$\bar{X} = 183.2$	$\bar{X} = 182.9$	$\bar{X} = 167.0$
1	% English	51.2	32.7	8.4
	% Spanish	1.3	17.9	32.4
	% Mixed	0.1	0.7	0.3
	% Non-verbal	47.4	48.7	58.9
	Mean frequency	$\bar{X} = 182.3$	$\bar{X} = 191.9$	$\bar{X} = 175.9$
2	% English	50.8	34.9	23.5
	% Spanish	1.8	13.7	28.8
	% Mixed	0.2	0.6	2.4
	% Non-verbal	47.2	50.8	45.2

What do teachers say?

Teacher utterances were coded into one of seven categories: (a) explaining—providing information; (b) questioning—asking students information; (c) commanding—directing students to do something; (d) modeling—demonstrating how something should be said; (e) feedback—informing students about their performance; (f) other—social comments such as, 'How are you today,' 'What a nice picture,' etc.; and (g) monitoring—teacher is not speaking at the time of observation, but is supervising students, such as during a test or seatwork.

Without considering the language used, with three exceptions, no clear differences in patterns emerge between programs or grade levels (see Table 6). The most common utterance types are the same for all three programs: question, command, explanation, and feedback. There are significant program differences with respect to proportion of explaining ($F = 5.92$, df $= 2$, $p = 0.0038$), commanding ($F = 9.61$, df $= 2$, $p = 0.0002$), and clarification questioning ($F = 4.34$, df $= 2$, $p = 0.0157$). The exceptions are that first grade late-exit teachers explain about half as much (11.7%) as do

TABLE 6 *Mean proportion of teacher behaviors by category, program and grade*

Pooled across languages

		Program		
Grade		Immersion strategy	Early-exit	Late-exit
	Mean frequency	$\bar{X} = 264.4$	$\bar{X} = 255.8$	$\bar{X} = 209.3$
1	% Explain	18.6	20.2	11.7
	% Question	23.6	23.2	19.9
	% Command	22.4	22.2	33.3
	% Modeling	3.5	4.3	3.0
	% Feedback	22.7	19.4	20.8
	% Other	1.2	1.7	0.9
	% Monitoring	8.0	8.9	10.5
	Mean frequency	$\bar{X} = 255.8$	$\bar{X} = 274.9$	$\bar{X} = 263.6$
2	% Explain	17.7	21.0	17.6
	% Question	24.7	22.8	22.8
	% Command	21.6	20.1	25.0
	% Modeling	3.3	3.8	2.3
	% Feedback	22.2	21.6	23.7
	% Other	0.9	1.3	0.6
	% Monitoring	9.6	9.5	8.2

For English only

		Program		
Grade		Immersion strategy	Early-exit	Late-exit
	Mean frequency	$\bar{X} = 232.2$	$\bar{X} = 154.4$	$\bar{X} = 41.7$
1	% Explain	20.2	21.5	17.3
	% Question	25.8	26.6	22.5
	% Command	24.1	25.1	38.5
	% Modeling	3.8	4.0	5.1
	% Feedback	24.9	20.6	16.4
	% Other	1.2	2.2	0.2
	% Monitoring	0.0	0.0	0.0

(*Continued*)

TABLE 6 *Continued*
For English only

Grade		Program		
		Immersion strategy	*Early-exit*	*Late-exit*
	Mean frequency	$\bar{X} = 224.3$	$\bar{X} = 186.8$	$\bar{X} = 111.2$
2	% Explain	19.9	22.5	16.7
	% Question	27.7	24.7	22.2
	% Command	23.6	22.2	27.5
	% Modeling	3.6	3.8	5.3
	% Feedback	24.1	24.5	28.1
	% Other	1.0	2.2	0.1
	% Monitoring	0.0	0.0	0.0

For Spanish only

Grade		Program		
		Immersion strategy	*Early-exit*	*Late-exit*
	Mean frequency	$\bar{X} = 4.4$	$\bar{X} = 73.6$	$\bar{X} = 137.8$
1	% Explain	5.6	18.2	12.1
	% Question	27.3	24.1	23.6
	% Command	32.6	19.6	35.6
	% Modeling	6.3	9.0	2.3
	% Feedback	28.3	24.4	25.3
	% Other	0.0	4.8	1.0
	% Monitoring	0.0	0.0	0.0
	Mean frequency	$\bar{X} = 5.9$	$\bar{X} = 64.7$	$\bar{X} = 132.7$
2	% Explain	23.4	21.2	19.5
	% Question	8.7	25.0	24.6
	% Command	37.8	20.8	28.5
	% Modeling	1.8	6.8	2.5
	% Feedback	28.4	25.1	24.5
	% Other	0.0	1.1	0.4
	% Monitoring	0.0	0.0	0.0

early-exit (20.2%) or immersion teachers (18.6%), and late-exit first grade teachers give about one-third more commands (33.3%) than do early-exit (22.2%) or immersion (22.4%) teachers and first grade immersion strategy (23.6%) and early-exit (23.2%) teachers ask more questions than do late-exit teachers (19.9%). In sum, the basic teaching behaviors appear to be equally present in about the same frequency across programs and grades.

Teaching behaviors are examined by language use to determine if teachers use English and Spanish differently. Table 6 provides the distribution of teacher utterances when English is spoken. As before, across programs and grades the primary teaching behaviors are questioning, feedback, explaining and commanding. Only slight differences are noted across grades within programs. Across programs and grade levels teachers tend to explain more as grade level increases.

Late-exit second grade teachers provide more feedback (28.1%) and fewer commands (27.2%) than do late-exit first grade teachers (16.4% and 38.5%, respectively). This probably reflects increased maturity and familiarity with school procedures among students from first grade to second grade.

When Spanish is considered, slight grade level differences within program as well as program-within-grade-level differences are noted (see Table 6). The low frequency of Spanish utterances by immersion strategy teachers should be kept in mind when considering this part of the table. The proportion of explanations increases (5.6% to 23.4%) as does commanding (32.6% to 37.8%) as grade level increases within the immersion program. A similar pattern occurs in the early-exit and late-exit bilingual program.

Comparing programs within grade level reveals that early-exit and late-exit teachers tend to be more similar in Spanish, with both differing somewhat from immersion strategy teachers. First grade immersion teachers explain less than their early-exit and late-exit counterparts. In the second grade the only major difference appears to be that immersion strategy teachers proportionately command more than do early-exit or late-exit second grade teachers; however, early-exit and late-exit second grade teachers question twice as much as do immersion strategy second grade teachers.

In sum, with one exception teachers in the three programs tend not to use English and Spanish differently. That is, teachers tend to make the same types of statements in both languages. Immersion strategy teachers are the exception. While they do not use much Spanish, when they do use it, they use it to provide students with feedback and give them commands.

Do teachers speak differently to limited-English-proficient students than to fluent-English-proficient and/or English-only speaking students?

A major assumption underlying the instruction of second language learners is that teachers need to differentiate their speech to students who are learning English (i.e. LEP students) from those students who are native speakers of English (i.e. EO students) or second language learners who have acquired sufficient proficiency in English to function as effectively as native speakers of English (i.e. FEP students). To determine if this differentiation occurs, teacher/student interactions were divided into three groups—teacher and LEP-only; teacher and FEP/EO-only; and teacher and LEP/FEP and/or EO mix. This was possible in that the language proficiency of the student or students with whom a teacher spoke was coded for each teacher utterance. The mean proportion of teacher behaviors was calculated by type of behavior, program, and grade for each of these three student groups. By comparing teacher behavior by grade within program with LEP-only, FEP/EO-only, and LEP/FEP and/or EO (see Table 7) students, we can determine whether teachers do say different things to each of these three student groups.

Two striking observations are noteworthy. The first is that with three exceptions, teachers within programs across grades do not appear to differentiate their speech when speaking to LEP-only or FEP/EO-only student groups (see Table 7). Early-exit and late-exit first and second grade teachers are the exception. Early-exit and late-exit first grade teachers give more commands to FEP/EO student groups (31.1% and 30.8% respectively) than do first grade immersion teachers (19.5%). The second exception is that early-exit first grade teachers give FEP and/or EO student groups more commands (31.1%) than they do to LEP-only students (20.3%). The third exception is that second grade late-exit teachers ask more questions of FEPs/EOs than they do of LEPs (32.8% vs. 24.4%). Otherwise, immersion and late-exit teachers consistently appear to make similar statements to LEP-only and FEP and/or EO students across grades.

The second most interesting, and somewhat baffling, finding is that while teachers across programs may not differentiate their speech between LEP-only and FEP and/or EO student groups, they pointedly do speak differently when interacting with LEP, FEP, and/or EO students mixed together (see Table 7). This appears to be consistent across programs by grade.

Immersion strategy first grade teachers explain more to mixed groups of students (39.4%) than they do to FEP and/or EO students (14.6%) or to LEP-only students (15.6%). Similarly, they do not ask as many questions of

TABLE 7 *Mean proportion of teacher behaviors (English and Spanish) to LEP, FEP/EO and mixed groups by type, program and grade*

To LEPs

Grade		Immersion strategy	Early-exit	Late-exit
			Program	
	Mean frequency	$\bar{X} = 191.9$	$\bar{X} = 178.4$	$\bar{X} = 144.3$
1	% Explain	15.6	17.5	9.7
	% Ask questions	27.4	28.2	23.2
	% Command	21.8	20.3	32.1
	% Modeling	2.5	3.3	2.4
	% Feedback	25.7	24.6	27.1
	% Other	1.3	1.3	1.1
	% Monitoring	5.7	4.8	4.4
	Mean frequency	$\bar{X} = 181.4$	$\bar{X} = 159.3$	$\bar{X} = 128.3$
2	% Explain	14.2	17.2	16.9
	% Ask questions	28.5	26.6	24.4
	% Command	20.8	20.6	23.5
	% Modeling	1.9	1.7	2.0
	% Feedback	27.6	27.9	28.9
	% Other	0.8	1.5	0.7
	% Monitoring	6.1	4.5	3.7

To FEPs/EOs

Grade		Immersion strategy	Early-exit	Late-exit
			Program	
	Mean frequency	$\bar{X} = 55.4$	$\bar{X} = 41.9$	$\bar{X} = 21.7$
1	% Explain	14.6	16.0	14.3
	% Ask questions	30.1	25.5	27.0
	% Command	19.5	31.1	30.8
	% Modeling	1.2	2.7	0.0
	% Feedback	31.9	23.3	25.6
	% Other	1.0	0.1	2.4
	% Monitoring	1.7	1.3	0.0

(*Continued*)

TABLE 7 *Continued*
To FEPs/EOs

Grade		Program		
		Immersion strategy	*Early-exit*	*Late-exit*
	Mean frequency	$\bar{X} = 50.4$	$\bar{X} = 55.1$	$\bar{X} = 74.4$
2	% Explain	12.1	13.0	12.3
	% Ask questions	31.9	31.6	32.8
	% Command	14.6	20.3	20.2
	% Modeling	1.2	0.3	0.7
	% Feedback	28.8	32.3	32.7
	% Other	1.0	0.7	0.4
	% Monitoring	10.5	1.9	0.9

To mixed groups (LEPs/FEPs/EOs)

Grade		Program		
		Immersion strategy	*Early-exit*	*Late-exit*
	Mean frequency	$\bar{X} = 87.8$	$\bar{X} = 74.2$	$\bar{X} = 65.0$
1	% Explain	39.4	27.5	10.8
	% Ask questions	13.8	11.5	9.1
	% Command	16.3	21.0	41.2
	% Modeling	6.0	7.1	4.5
	% Feedback	9.3	6.1	3.4
	% Other	1.6	4.0	0.5
	% Monitoring	13.6	22.8	30.6
	Mean frequency	$\bar{X} = 84.9$	$\bar{X} = 99.0$	$\bar{X} = 68.8$
2	% Explain	29.3	31.1	26.5
	% Ask questions	18.2	12.1	13.6
	% Command	20.8	22.4	26.0
	% Modeling	5.9	7.3	2.6
	% Feedback	6.8	7.4	11.2
	% Other	1.1	0.1	0.3
	% Monitoring	17.8	19.6	19.8

mixed groups (13.8%), as compared to FEP and/or EO (30.1%) or LEP-only (27.4%) student groups. Interestingly, more modeling is provided to mixed groups (6.0%) than to FEP and/or EO (1.2%) or LEP-only (2.5%) students. Mixed groups of students do not receive as much teacher feedback (9.3%) as do FEP and/or EO (31.9%) or LEP-only (25.7%) students. Finally, first grade immersion strategy teachers spend more time monitoring mixed groups of students (13.6%) than they do FEP and/or EO (1.7%) or LEP-only (5.7%) student groups. A somewhat similar pattern occurs among early-exit first grade teachers.

Early-exit first grade teachers provide more explanation to mixed groups of students (27.5%) than they do to either FEP and/or EO only students (16.0%) or to LEP-only students (17.5%). However, mixed student groups do not receive as many questions (11.5%) as do FEP and/or EO (25.5%) or LEP-only (28.2%) students. As with the immersion strategy teachers, early-exit first grade teachers provide more modeling to mixed groups of students (21.0%) than to either FEP and/or EO students (2.7%) or to LEP-only students (3.3%). Similarly, early-exit first grade teachers, like their immersion strategy counterparts, do more monitoring of mixed student groups (22.8%) than they do of either FEP and/or EO (1.3%) or of LEP-only (4.8%) students.

With the exception of the first grade, late-exit second grade teachers also provide almost twice as many explanations to mixed student groups (26.5%) as compared to FEP and/or EO (12.3%) or LEP-only (16.9%) students. Across grade levels late-exit teachers ask fewer questions when speaking to mixed groups of students than they do of FEP and/or EO-only or LEP-only student groups. As in the other two programs, all late-exit teachers provide more modeling to mixed student groups than to either FEP and/or EO or LEP-only groups.

In sum, it appears that teachers in all three programs tend to provide more explanations when speaking to mixed groups of students than when speaking to LEP-only or FEP and/or EO students. This may reflect the teacher's concern that he/she must take extra pains to ensure that the LEP student is following the discussion in a mixed setting. Whereas when LEP students are separated, presumably the teacher's statements to them can be more directed to their level of understanding. Similarly, teachers in all three programs seem to prefer to ask more questions when students are separated by language status (LEP-only or FEP and/or EO) than when they are mixed. This may be reasonable in that, given the differences in language proficiency among students, certain types of questions (such as referential when speaking in Spanish and display when speaking in English) might be more appropriate for LEP students and others for FEP and/or EO students (referential questions when using English). Modeling appears to be something that teachers prefer to do with mixed groups of students. This also is reasonable in that in a modeling situation one can easily mix students, and, given the expected repetition, all students can participate equally. Similarly, teachers tend to monitor mixed groups of students in all three programs more than they do LEP-only or FEP and/or EO student groups. Once again, monitoring occurs more frequently during periods of whole class instruction rather than small group instruction. As such, students will tend to be mixed. Thus, teachers in all three programs do exhibit some sensitivity to the special needs of LEP students when they are mixed with FEP and/or EO students.

What do teachers talk about?

Whenever teachers initiated a conversation with students, the focus of their conversation was coded as form (i.e. how language is used), concept (i.e. expressing an idea), or non-verbal (i.e. whenever gestures were used to communicate with students). The data suggest that the majority of teacher-initiated conversations with students across programs and grade levels focus on concepts (65.6% to 77.7%) (see Table 8). Teacher initiations that focus on form range from 8.8% to 18.0%. Teachers use gestures to communicate with students from 13.6% to 17.4% of the time. This pattern also holds true whether teachers use English or Spanish (see Table 8). This pattern is desirable for language learning in that evidence suggests that in the early stages of language development, language learning is facilitated when the focus is on the communication of meaning (i.e. what is said) rather than how language should be used (i.e. how it is said).

TABLE 8 *Mean proportion of teacher initiations by focus, program, grade and language*

English and Spanish

		Program	
Grade	Immersion strategy	Early-exit	Late-exit
Mean frequency	$\bar{X} = 150.5$	$\bar{X} = 145.4$	$\bar{X} = 146.7$
1 % Form	18.0	17.3	9.2
% Concept	67.1	65.6	74.1
% Non-verbal	14.9	17.1	16.7

TABLE 8 *Continued*
English and Spanish

Grade		Program		
		Immersion strategy	Early-exit	Late-exit
	Mean frequency	$\bar{X} = 149.3$	$\bar{X} = 160.4$	$\bar{X} = 151.7$
2	% Form	15.4	14.3	8.8
	% Concept	67.2	69.0	77.7
	% Non-verbal	17.4	16.8	13.6

English only

Grade		Program		
		Immersion strategy	Early-exit	Late-exit
	Mean frequency	$\bar{X} = 123.9$	$\bar{X} = 82.9$	$\bar{X} = 30.8$
1	% Form	21.2	16.3	7.6
	% Concept	78.8	83.7	92.4
	Mean frequency	$\bar{X} = 121.8$	$\bar{X} = 100.8$	$\bar{X} = 60.6$
2	% Form	18.4	14.8	14.3
	% Concept	81.6	85.2	85.7

Spanish only

Grade		Program		
		Immersion strategy	Early-exit	Late-exit
	Mean frequency	$\bar{X} = 3.5$	$\bar{X} = 40.5$	$\bar{X} = 89.0$
1	% Form	15.9	27.9	10.9
	% Concept	84.1	72.1	89.1
	Mean frequency	$\bar{X} = 3.9$	$\bar{X} = 34.9$	$\bar{X} = 75.5$
2	% Form	3.9	21.9	9.5
	% Concept	96.1	78.1	90.5

When language is not considered, significant program differences are noted ($F = 9.92$, df $= 2$, $p = 0.0001$). Across grades proportionately more teacher initiations on form occur among immersion strategy and early-exit classrooms than among late-exit classrooms. While not significant, minor grade level differences within programs are noted. Immersion strategy teachers initiate conversations less on form as grade level increases. Presumably this reflects the increased language skills among students as they get older. A similar trend is observed among early-exit and late-exit teachers. The proportion of teacher initiations among early-exit and late-exit teachers on form decreases from first (17.3% and 9.2%, respectively) to second grade (14.3% and 8.8% respectively).

When language is considered, teachers do use English and Spanish differently. Simply looking at the mean frequency, one finds that both immersion and early-exit teachers typically use English when initiating a conversation with students across grade levels. Among late-exit teachers, the frequency of teacher-initiated conversation in English increases as grade level increases.

When grade levels within programs are examined, language differences emerge. There is a steady increase in the proportion of teacher initiations in English and Spanish dealing with concepts as grade level increases. Early-exit teachers appear to focus more on form in Spanish in first grade (27.9%) and second grade (21.9%) than on form in English (16.3% and 14.8%, respectively). Late-exit teachers tend to increase conversations in English related to form as grade level increases from first (7.6%) to second grade (14.3%). Late-exit teachers appear to be more consistent in their initiation of form-related conversations in Spanish, from 10.9% in first grade to 9.5% in second grade. The patterns of teacher behavior by language are consistent with the instructional models of early-exit and late-exit programs. The limited use of Spanish by some immersion teachers is also evidence that the immersion teachers are consistent with their program model.

What types of questions do teachers ask?

Questioning, the second most frequently occurring teacher behavior, was coded in three ways to describe the nature of information sought from the students. One count coded the frequency with which the student was asked for previously learned information (i.e. display question—what is two times two? What happened to Humpty Dumpty?), for new information (i.e. referential questions—How many ways can you use a newspaper? How are you feeling today?), or for information to confirm/clarify what was said or understood (i.e. What did you say? Can you tell us in your own words?). Disregarding the language used, the patterns were consistent across programs and grade levels. Notwithstanding, there were significant program differences in the proportion of clarification questions made ($F = 4.34$, df = 2, $p = 0.0157$) with first grade immersion strategy teachers providing more than either early- or late-exit teachers. Moreover, there was a significant program grade interaction effect with respect to the proportion of referential questions made ($F = 4.74$, df = 2, $p = 0.0110$). This reflects the slight increases in referential questions as grade level increases among late-exit and immersion strategy teachers. In general, two to three times as many display questions were asked for every referential question (see Table 9). This pattern would suggest that most teacher questioning consists of simple information recall. Research indicates greater student achievement is realized in classrooms where higher-order, more cognitively demanding questions are more evident than are repetitive recall-type questions (Redfield & Rousseau, 1981). These patterns would suggest less demanding instructional environments.

Differences in the types of questions asked by language raise further questions about the instructional demands of each of the three programs (see Table 9). With one exception immersion strategy, early-exit and late-exit teachers are somewhat similar in their questions in English and to some extent in Spanish. Approximately two-thirds (61.5%) to over three-fourths (78.8%) of all questions are display. The exception occurs in first grade early-exit classrooms wherein slightly more than half (56.8%) of teacher questions in English-only are display. However, second grade late-exit program teachers resemble the questioning pattern of immersion strategy and early-exit teachers when English is used.

When Spanish is considered, first grade immersion strategy teachers ask more referential (68.3%) and clarification (10.0%) questions than in English (27.7% and 3.1%, respectively). However, since these numbers are based on an unusually low frequency of questions ($\bar{X} = 3.2$), these numbers are difficult to interpret. In contrast, second grade immersion teachers also ask fewer referential questions in Spanish (25.0%) than in English (32.8%). Early-exit questioning patterns are similar to those in late-exit classrooms, following a two to one ratio of display to referential questions, with the exception of the first grade where it is more nearly equal (56.8% display to 40.5% referential). Across grade levels, late-exit teachers ask the same types of questions in English as in Spanish. As in English, late-exit teachers tend to ask more display than clarification questions when Spanish is used.

Overall, the data suggest that, regardless of the language used, teachers typically ask primarily information recall questions, rather than more analytical cognitively demanding questions (i.e. When was the Gutenberg press invented? vs. Why was the invention of the Gutenberg press so

TABLE 9 *Mean proportion of teacher questions by type, program and grade*

English and Spanish

		Program		
Grade		Immersion strategy	Early-exit	Late-exit
	Mean frequency	$\bar{X} = 62.6$	$\bar{X} = 60.2$	$\bar{X} = 41.3$
1	% Display	68.8	59.5	76.6
	% Referential	28.0	37.6	22.9
	% Clarification	3.1	2.9	0.5
	Mean frequency	$\bar{X} = 62.3$	$\bar{X} = 62.3$	$\bar{X} = 60.5$
2	% Display	63.2	69.0	65.4
	% Referential	33.1	28.9	33.1
	% Clarification	3.7	2.1	1.5

English only

		Program		
Grade		Immersion strategy	Early-exit	Late-exit
	Mean frequency	$\bar{X} = 60.0$	$\bar{X} = 40.3$	$\bar{X} = 9.0$
1	% Display	69.2	56.8	71.7
	% Referential	27.7	40.5	22.7
	% Clarification	3.1	2.8	5.6
	Mean frequency	$\bar{X} = 61.3$	$\bar{X} = 46.4$	$\bar{X} = 33.3$
2	% Display	63.5	66.1	61.5
	% Referential	32.8	31.1	36.7
	% Clarification	3.7	2.8	1.8

TABLE 9 *Continued*
Spanish only

Grade		Program		
		Immersion strategy	*Early-exit*	*Late-exit*
	Mean frequency	$\bar{X} = 3.2$	$\bar{X} = 24.0$	$\bar{X} = 31.8$
1	% Display	21.7	61.4	76.0
	% Referential	68.3	35.5	24.0
	% Clarification	10.0	3.1	0.0
	Mean frequency	$\bar{X} = 8.0$	$\bar{X} = 17.3$	$\bar{X} = 32.9$
2	% Display	70.8	78.8	64.9
	% Referential	25.0	19.0	33.0
	% Clarification	4.2	2.2	2.1

important?). One positive note is that, when first grade immersion strategy teachers use Spanish, they tend to use it for clarification to make sure that a child is understanding the lesson. As the proportion of referential questions decreases rather than increases, it appears that teachers in the immersion strategy program do not adjust their use of English to the language proficiency level of their limited-English proficient students.

Do teachers shelter their language through the use of realia?

Realia refers to pictures, pantomime, models, etc., any strategy or device that a teacher might use along with what is being said to help the second language learner 'understand the meaning' of the verbal message. For example, the teacher points to a color chart and says, 'This is the color orange' while the corresponding color is pointed out. Or the teacher says, 'Run', and he/she begins running. Realia is not widely used in any of the three programs (see Table 10).

In sum, there is little evidence of teacher attempts to adjust their behaviors (i.e. through the use of realia) to accommodate the needs of second language learners among immersion strategy, early-exit, and late-exit programs.

TABLE 10 *Mean proportion of teacher use of realia by program and grade*

Grade		Program		
		Immersion strategy	Early-exit	Late-exit
	Mean frequency	$\bar{X} = 175.3$	$\bar{X} = 172.0$	$\bar{X} = 163.7$
1	% Used	4.7	8.7	1.5
	% Not used	95.3	91.3	98.3
	% Unknown	0.0	0.0	0.2
	Mean frequency	$\bar{X} = 173.8$	$\bar{X} = 183.8$	$\bar{X} = 170.5$
2	% Used	4.1	4.2	0.9
	% Not Used	95.9	95.8	99.1
	% Unknown	0.0	0.0	0.0

What do students say?

Whenever students initiated a conversation, their behaviors were coded into one of four categories: (a) asking a question (What time do we have lunch?); (b) making a free comment (the teacher mentions that Christopher Columbus was from Italy; student pipes up and says, 'my Uncle Paolo is from Italy.'); (c) non-verbal (student makes no verbal statement, but makes a gesture to initiate a conversation, such as raising his hand for the teacher's attention); and (d) other (verbal statements used to initiate a conversation that could not be coded in one of the other three categories, such as 'Mrs. Juarez, kick the ball with your right foot.').

Without considering language, across programs and grades students initiate a conversation by asking a question or by making a free comment (see Table 11). Gestures are rarely used by students in any program to initiate a conversation. First grade immersion students make more free comments (51.2%) than do first grade students in early-exit (38.5%) or late-exit (48.2%) programs. In contrast, late-exit first graders start a conversation with questions (45.1%) slightly more often than do first graders in early-exit (38.6%) or immersion strategy programs (36.4%). No striking differences in verbal statements occur between second grade immersion strategy or early-exit students. Roughly, students tend to initiate

TABLE 11 *Mean proportion of student initiating behaviors by type, function, program and grade*

English and Spanish

		Program		
Grade		Immersion strategy	Early-exit	Late-exit
	Mean frequency	$\bar{X} = 24.8$	$\bar{X} = 26.6$	$\bar{X} = 17.0$
1	% Ask question	36.4	38.6	45.1
	% Free comment	51.2	38.5	48.2
	% Non-verbal	11.8	18.8	5.8
	% Other	0.6	4.1	0.9
	Mean frequency	$\bar{X} = 24.5$	$\bar{X} = 23.4$	$\bar{X} = 18.7$
2	% Ask question	42.8	38.2	56.4
	% Free comment	44.6	47.1	33.1
	% Non-verbal	11.8	10.5	8.9
	% Other	0.9	4.3	1.5

English only

		Program		
Grade		Immersion strategy	Early-exit	Late-exit
	Mean frequency	$\bar{X} = 21.1$	$\bar{X} = 16.0$	$\bar{X} = 2.4$
1	% Ask question	43.2	49.5	26.7
	% Free comment	56.0	45.9	73.3
	% Non-verbal	0.0	0.0	0.0
	% Other	0.7	4.6	0.0
	Mean frequency	$\bar{X} = 19.8$	$\bar{X} = 15.4$	$\bar{X} = 8.4$
2	% Ask question	48.8	46.3	60.4
	% Free comment	50.3	49.1	36.7
	% Non-verbal	0.0	0.0	0.0
	% Other	0.9	4.6	2.9

(*Continued*)

TABLE 11 *Continued*
Spanish only

		Program	
Grade	Immersion strategy	Early-exit	Late-exit
Mean frequency	$\bar{X} = 2.2$	$\bar{X} = 7.3$	$\bar{X} = 13.5$
1 % Ask question	7.4	36.7	45.5
% Free comment	92.6	59.8	53.4
% Non-verbal	0.0	0.0	0.0
% Other	0.0	3.6	1.1
Mean frequency	$\bar{X} = 4.4$	$\bar{X} = 7.3$	$\bar{X} = 9.2$
2 % Ask question	51.3	26.0	68.8
% Free comment	48.7	71.8	30.6
% Non-verbal	0.0	0.0	0.0
% Other	0.0	2.2	0.6

a conversation more by asking questions as grade level increases in all programs. This may reflect increased classroom structure and teacher disapproval of free comments as grade level increases. No clear patterns emerge when student initiating behaviors are examined by language. When all student behaviors are considered, there is a significant program by grade interaction with respect to the proportion of non-verbal behaviors mode ($F = 4.45$, df $= 2, p = 0.0141$). While the proportion of non-verbal behaviors remains the same for first and second grade immersion students, it markedly decreases among early-exit but increases among late-exit students.

What do students say when they respond to teacher initiations?

Student responses to teacher initiations were coded into one of nine categories. Four of them are the same as those defined earlier for student initiation: asking questions, making a free comment, non-verbal and other. The remaining codes included: (a) repetition (student response to a teacher statement modeling how something is said, usually occurring during a drill): (b) expected response (student attempts to give the single 'right' answer in response to a question, such as 'What is two times two?' or 'who was the first president of the United States?,' although his response may actually be incorrect); (c) free response (student responds to an open-ended question, such as 'What would you do with a million dollars?'); (d) no response (the student, not hearing the teacher, does not acknowledge the teacher's initiation bid); and (e) listening (the student is listening to a teacher's presentation).

When language is not considered, consistently across programs and grades the most prevalent student responses were expected responses and non-verbal (see Table 12). In fact, there are significant grade level differences in the proportion of non-verbal behaviors made ($F = 6.89$, df $= 1$,

TABLE 12 *Mean proportion of student responding behaviors by type, program and grade*

		Program		
Grade		Immersion strategy	Early-exit	Late-exit
	Mean frequency	$\bar{X} = 150.5$	$\bar{X} = 145.4$	$\bar{X} = 146.7$
1	% Ask question	1.0	0.7	0.6
	% Repetition	5.0	6.3	3.1
	% Expected response	32.5	27.6	27.0
	% Free response	5.5	9.7	3.3
	% Free comment	2.3	2.2	1.0
	% Non-verbal	42.4	44.7	61.3
	% No response	4.6	3.9	2.5
	% Other	0.0	0.0	0.0
	% Listening	6.9	4.9	1.2
	Mean frequency	$\bar{X} = 149.3$	$\bar{X} = 160.4$	$\bar{X} = 151.7$
2	% Ask question	1.0	0.6	0.6
	% Repetition	3.8	3.4	3.2
	% Expected response	32.2	31.3	35.5
	% Free response	7.4	5.6	7.7
	% Free comment	2.4	1.6	3.0
	% Non-verbal	43.2	43.5	40.2
	% No response	4.2	5.8	3.9
	% Other	0.0	0.0	0.0
	% Listening	5.7	8.3	6.0

$p = 0.0029$) as well as a significant program by grade interaction with respect to the proportion of non-verbal behaviors ($F = 6.22$, df $= 2$, $p = 0.0029$). The high frequency of expected responses (27.0%–35.5%) reflects that display questions are one of the most frequent ways in which teachers initiate conversations with students. Although there is a significant program by grade interaction with respect to the proportion of free responses ($F = 4.99$, df $= 2$, $p = 0.0087$), the frequency of this behavior is quite low (3.3% – 9.7%). The high frequency of non-verbal student responses (40.2% – 61.3%), along with listening (1.2% – 8.3%) and no responses (2.5% – 5.8%), dramatically underscores the passiveness of students' interactions with teachers. From a language development perspective, we have already noted that information recall does not facilitate the acquisition of higher language learning as much as more active referential questioning. We also noted earlier that it is important that students produce language if they are to develop language. These two patterns of student responses suggest that students in all three programs appear to have the opportunity for developing receptive language skills, but that the opportunities for developing productive language skills may be restricted.

When language is considered, the distribution of student responses changes dramatically. This largely reflects the coding procedures. All student behaviors were coded by language—English, Spanish, both English and Spanish, and none (no language). All non-verbal, no response, and listening responses by definition are non-language. As such, when only those student responses in English-only or Spanish-only are coded, all non-language behaviors are omitted from the analysis, as are student responses wherein both English and Spanish were used. Consequently, Tables 13 and 14 do not include any non-language student responses or those wherein both English and Spanish were used concomitantly. While student response 'other' is a verbal statement, its frequency was so low that it was dropped from the analysis. Consequently, only five of the nine student behaviors are included in Tables 13 and 14.

Table 13 presents the data for student responses in English. Once again, across programs and grades the most frequent student response is expected responses. Also, expected responses tend to increase as grade increases. Expected responses are followed by either repetition or free responses. With one exception, there are no striking differences between immersion strategy and early-exit students by program or grade level. First grade is the exception; first grade early-exit students make more free responses (26.2%) and fewer expected responses (54.9%) when using English than do immersion strategy students (11.7% and 70.5%, respectively). This pattern reflects the higher use of referential questions which require a free

TABLE 13 *Mean proportion of student responding behaviors in English by type, program and grade*

Grade		Immersion strategy	Early-exit	Late-exit
			Program	
	Mean frequency	$\bar{X} = 68.5$	$\bar{X} = 42.8$	$\bar{X} = 12.0$
1	% Ask question	2.7	1.5	3.3
	% Repetition	10.5	11.3	21.6
	% Expected response	70.5	54.9	65.2
	% Free response	11.7	26.2	4.9
	% Free comment	4.7	6.2	4.9
	Mean frequency	$\bar{X} = 68.2$	$\bar{X} = 48.4$	$\bar{X} = 40.5$
2	% Ask question	2.1	1.1	0.7
	% Repetition	8.2	7.5	7.0
	% Expected response	70.1	71.5	67.7
	% Free response	14.7	15.7	18.4
	% Free comment	4.9	4.2	6.2

response by first grade early-exit teachers than by their immersion counterparts. However, late-exit first graders repeat more (21.6%) and make fewer free responses (4.9%) than do either immersion strategy (10.5% and 11.7%, respectively) or early-exit (11.3% and 26.2%, respectively) students. While late-exit first graders also make fewer expected responses (65.2%) than do first graders in immersion strategy (70.5%), they make more than do early-exit students (54.9%).

When student responses in Spanish are examined, as before, the most frequent student response is expected response (see Table 14). While the proportion of expected responses tends to increase with grade, the pattern is inconsistent, fluctuating from grade to grade within program. The low frequency of student responses in Spanish is so low that the distribution is not very useful. Noteworthy is that first grade early-exit students make more free responses (21.9%) and fewer expected responses (59.0%) than do late-exit students (10.9% and 80.4%, respectively) when Spanish is used.

In sum, the pattern of student responses suggests a less than optimum environment for developing oral language skills in all three programs from

TABLE 14 *Mean proportion of student responding behaviors in Spanish by type, program and grade*

Grade		Program		
		Immersion strategy	Early-exit	Late-exit
	Mean frequency	$\bar{X} = 1.8$	$\bar{X} = 30.7$	$\bar{X} = 38.8$
1	% Ask question	0.0	2.0	1.4
	% Repetition	20.0	13.7	5.0
	% Expected response	40.0	59.0	80.4
	% Free response	32.5	21.9	10.9
	% Free comment	7.5	3.3	2.3
	Mean frequency	$\bar{X} = 4.8$	$\bar{X} = 20.8$	$\bar{X} = 42.2$
2	% Ask question	2.4	1.2	1.6
	% Repetition	3.5	11.3	7.2
	% Expected response	64.1	78.0	71.3
	% Free response	30.0	6.8	13.8
	% Free comment	0.0	2.7	6.1

the perspective of having students produce language, be it in English or Spanish.

How often do students initiate a conversation with their teacher?

Consistently across programs and grades, the majority of student utterances (75.4% to 78.4%) are in response to teacher initiations (see Table 15). Student initiated utterances are generally less than one-fourth of all teacher–student exchanges in immersion strategy (23.3%–24.6%), early-exit (23.7%–24.0%), or late-exit (21.6%–23.2%) classrooms.

Do classroom processes differentiate programs? school districts? teachers?

Except for the extent to which English and Spanish are used in classrooms for instruction, case cluster analyses did not identify any classroom processes unique to each of the three program models, school districts, or teachers. The data show that classrooms fall on a continuum

TABLE 15 *Mean proportion of student utterances by type, program and grade*

		Program		
Grade		Immersion strategy	Early-exit	Late-exit
1	Mean frequency	$\bar{X} = 92.0$	$\bar{X} = 89.3$	$\bar{X} = 66.8$
	% Student initiated	23.3	23.7	23.2
	% Student response	76.7	76.3	76.8
2	Mean frequency	$\bar{X} = 91.3$	$\bar{X} = 89.1$	$\bar{X} = 97.4$
	% Student initiated	24.6	24.0	21.6
	% Student response	75.4	76.0	78.4

with respect to the distribution of any of the teacher behaviors examined. There is no clear clustering of teacher behaviors unique to programs, school districts, or teachers.

What is the relationship of those classroom processes examined?

Variable clustering techniques were used to reduce the number of variables. These techniques also allowed us to establish the extent to which certain behaviors and languages tended to occur together. The case clusters were based on the language used and on the various behaviors. In sum, the variable clustering analyses indicated that each of the teacher behaviors might be best viewed as separate aspects of the classroom, and that we should continue to be cautious whenever we combine, say, display questions and referential questions into a single 'questions' category. That is, teacher behaviors did not tend to be highly enough associated to be considered to be measuring the same construct. The case clustering analysis confirmed that the classrooms in the study could be divided into three natural groups based on the proportion of English used in the classroom, with these natural groups corresponding closely with the three program models. To explore the possibility that the various behaviors could be used to divide classrooms into natural groups without considering the language used, the case clustering was performed again omitting the percentage English variable. This analysis strongly indicated there were no natural groups or clusters among the classrooms when considering only the behavior variables.

Which of these classroom processes are associated with increased student initiated exchanges and overall student production?

Through the use of multiple regression techniques we attempted to predict the overall proportion of teacher–student exchanges that were student initiated and to predict the proportion of teacher–student exchanges that involved student language production. As predictor variables, we included each teacher-initiated behavior as a proportion of all teacher-initiated behaviors as well as the function (i.e. instruction, discipline, procedures, and miscellaneous), focus (i.e. form, content, or none) of the exchange as well as the following aspects of the context of the exchange: student activity (i.e. presentation, discussion, seatwork, drill, listening, interim, oral reading, and 'other'), realia (i.e. yes or no), and content area (i.e. reading language, math, social studies, non-academic, other academic, and procedures) as a proportion of teacher-initiated exchanges. We performed several stepwise regression analyses on each dependent variable. The regression analyses indicated that student initiation is more likely to occur in less structured classrooms, or those where we observed during seatwork or interim activities such as collecting lunch money. However, only 25% of the variance could be accounted for.

Prediction of student verbalization was considerably more successful. The overall conclusion was that teacher explanations and presentations as well as teacher monitoring and seatwork tend to result in relatively lower student verbalization, while teacher referential questions and drill result in relatively higher student verbalization.

Discussion

In summing up the findings of this study, we will focus on two issues, program differences and similarities in classroom language and the identification of those variables which led to high student initiations and verbalizations.

The most salient difference is the expected one. Language clearly differentiated the three program models and in accordance with the program model descriptions. This result is more significant than it appears on the surface, given the difficulty that bilingual programs in the United States have had in implementing any bilingual program model in which L1 is used to a significant degree (Legarreta, 1977; Wong Fillmore et al., 1985). This adherence to an articulated model validates the systematic procedure used in selecting participating school districts as study sites.

At this state our analyses of the patterns of classroom talk in terms of language are preliminary. We have not yet fully explored, for example, the link between these patterns and achievement. Nor have we investigated patterns of language use in detail. How often, for example, do switches from one language to another occur? We have preliminary results which indicate that the patterns of separation are different across programs. In immersion classrooms English is used over longer periods of time before there is a switch to Spanish (grade 1, 38.6 minutes; grade 2, 45.7 minutes). In contrast, early-exit classroom teachers switch from English to Spanish after 22.5 minutes in grade 1 and after 25.1 minutes in grade 2. In late-exit, switches from English to Spanish are more frequent, occurring after 6.3 minutes in grade 1 and after 17.3 minutes in grade 2 on the average. Research indicates that effective bilingual classroom teachers separate the two languages and do not use concurrent translation (Legarreta, 1979; Swain, 1983; Milk, 1986). Future analyses will identify those teachers who were most successful in separating the languages over longer periods of time and relate these patterns to achievement.

We now turn to a discussion of what appears to influence student output, specifically student initiations and verbalizations in general. It is important here to recall that it is in the nature of mainstream U.S. classrooms to allocate to the teacher the role of gate-keeper for classroom talk. Researchers using both interaction and discourse analyses have documented the preponderance of teacher talk in the classroom. Thus it is not surprising that students in all three program models tend to be passive and contribute little to classroom discussion. However, the nature of this passivity as Long (1983) points out may be of a different nature than that of mainstream students. Students with a limited proficiency in English may face considerable difficulties in responding even in situations in which fluent English speakers would have no difficulty whatsoever (Schinke-Llano, 1983: 157). Alternatively, the difference could be cultural, based on a dissonant perception of when it is appropriate to talk (Phillips, 1972).

In this study, three principal factors positively influenced student verbalizations: teachers' use of referential questions, drill and academic content other than math, reading or language arts, i.e. science, music or art. Teacher explaining and monitoring and activities such as seatwork, present-ation and transitional procedures such as taking roll reduced the likelihood of student verbalization. The exceptionally high proportion of display questions in contrast to referential questions has been documented in beginning ESL classes with adults (Long & Sato, 1983). Referential questions were rare in classroom discourse of six ESL lessons (14%), but in the majority in informal native to non-native speaker conversations (76%).

Since this type of question is, by its very nature, communicative and designed to elicit genuine information, it is not surprising that it should be so successful in generating student verbalization. Drill, an activity which assumes discourse rules of frequent give and take, as would be expected also generates student verbalization. Academic content which tends to involve the use of a more open ended format, where discourse rules are more fluid, i.e. science, music and art, also led to high levels of student participation. This type of content has been recently highlighted as offering much potential for student interaction in a second language context (Krashen, 1982). Behaviors and activities where discourse rules are generally more rigid, on the other hand, tend to be negatively related to student verbalizations. Thus, explaining, monitoring, seatwork, interim activities and presentation tend to not co-occur with high levels of student participation.

Implications of findings to classroom research and teaching practices

The procedures used to observe classrooms in this study have the advantage of capturing classroom interaction in large numbers of classrooms. For the purpose of the evaluation of program effects in large numbers of children, such an approach is pragmatically justified. It provides for the possibility of establishing a link between program classroom practice to intervening student behaviors which may then be linked to student achievement through more complex statistical analyses. This final step awaits the final analyses of the longitudinal study. However, such an approach is also limited in what it can say very specifically about the nature of classroom discourse. Data from the first year of data collection recorded on audiotape will allow for further analyses of a more detailed nature. The advantages of ethnographic data collection techniques cannot be realized through this approach, however. Such is the nature of research, which dictates the selection of some questions while it forces us to forgo others. Thus the findings of this study contribute to our knowledge about classroom process but leave many remaining questions beyond the scope of the study design. How, for example, do classrooms which make use of cooperative techniques differ in their effectiveness in promoting student verbalization? Within program models, how do teachers successful in promoting student achievement differ in their classroom behavior from those who are less successful? What adjustments in register are the most effective in promoting student participation?

Teachers involved in the instruction of LEP students can take these findings as additional reinforcement to current theoretical views of what makes second language acquisition work. Certain classroom practices appear to be strongly linked to student verbalization. Krashen (1981), Swain (1983) and Long (1983), all view student verbalization as necessary for second language acquisition to take place, although each from a somewhat different perspective. However, this research cannot at this juncture give a recipe for what a good teacher should do. It can only suggest what may seem worth trying and validating through personal experience. Teachers in bilingual programs should be encouraged by the evidence that some bilingual programs do in fact use the L1 of the students despite the pressures in our society against it.

References

BAKER, K and DEKANTER, A.A. 1981, *Effectiveness of Bilingual Education: A Review of the Literature*. Washington, DC: Department of Education, Office of Planning, Budget and Evaluation.

CHAUDRON, C. 1977, A descriptive model of discourse in the corrective treatment of learner's errors. *Language Learning* 27, 29–46.

—— 1979, Complexity of ESL teachers' speech and vocabulary expansion elaboration. Paper presented at 13th Annual TESOL Convention, Boston, MA.

—— 1985, *Coding Procedures and Guidelines for SRA Project*. Mountain View, CA: SRA Technologies/Second Language Research.

COHEN, A.D. 1975, Error correction and the training of language teachers. *The Modern Language Journal* 59, 414–22.

DUNKIN, M.J. and BIDDLE, B.J. 1974, *The Study of Teaching*. New York: Holt, Rinehart & Winston.

GAIES, S.J. 1977, The nature of linguistic input in formal second language learning: Linguistic and communicative strategies in ESL teachers' classroom language. In H.D. BROWN, C.A. YORIO and R.H. CRYMES (eds), *On TESOL, '77. Teaching and Learning English as a Second Language: Trends in Research and Practice*. Washington, DC: TESOL.

HAMAYAN, E. and TUCKER, G.R. 1980, Language input in the bilingual classroom and its relationship to second language achievement. *TESOL Quarterly* 14, 453–68.

HERNANDEZ-CHAVEZ, E. 1984, The inadequacy of English immersion education as an educational approach for language minority students in the United States. In *Studies on Immersion Education: A Collection for United States Educators*. Sacramento, CA: California State Department of Education.

HOLLEY, F.M. and KING, J.K. 1971, Imitation and correction in foreign language learning. *The Modern Language Journal* 55, 494–8.

KRASHEN, S. 1981, The 'fundamental pedagogical principle' in second language teaching. *Studia Linguistica* 35, (1–2), 50–70.

——1982, *Principles and Practice in Second Language Acquisition*. New York, NY: Pergamon Press.

LEGARRETA, D. 1977, Language choice in bilingual classrooms. *TESOL Quarterly* 1, 9–16.

—— 1979, The effects of program models on language acquisition by Spanish speaking children. *TESOL Quarterly* 13, 521–34.

LONG, M. 1981, Input, interaction, and second language acquisition. In H. WINITZ (ed.), *Native Language and Foreign Language Acquisition*. New York, NY: New York Academy of Sciences.

—— 1983, Inside the 'Black Box': Methodological issues in classroom research on language learning. In H. SELIGER and M. LONG (eds), *Classroom Oriented Research in Second Language Acquisition*. Rowley, MA: Newbury House.

LONG, M. and SATO, C. 1983, Classroom foreigner talk discourses: forms and functions of teacher's questions. In H. SELIGER and M. LONG (eds), *Classroom Oriented Research in Second Language Acquisition*. Rowely, MA: Newbury House Publishers.

MACKEY, W. 1972, *Bilingual Education in a Binational School*. Rowley, MA: Newbury House.

MILK, R. 1980, Variation in language use patterns across different group settings in two bilingual second grade classrooms. Unpublished Doctoral Dissertation, Stanford University, Stanford, CA.

—— 1986, The issue of language separation in bilingual methodology. In E. GARCIA and B. FLORES (eds), *Language and Literacy Research in Bilingual Education*. ASU Press.

MOOS, R. 1976, *The Human Context: Environmental Determinants of Behavior*. New York, NY: John Wiley & Sons.

NERENZ, A. and KNOP, C. 1983, Allocated time, curricular content, and student engagement outcomes in the second language classroom. *Canadian Modern Language Review* 39, 222–32.

OMAGGIO, A. 1982, The relationship between personalized classroom talk and teacher effectiveness ratings: Some research results. *Foreign Language Annals* 15, 255–69.

PEÑA-HUGHES, E. and SOLIS, J. 1980, ABCs (Unpublished report). McAllen, TX: McAllen Independent School District.

PHILIPS, S. 1972, Participant structures and communicative competence: Warmsprings children in community and classroom. In D. CAZDEN, V. JOHN and D. HYMES (eds), *Functions of Language in the Classroom*. New York, NY: Teachers College Press, Columbia University.

POLITZER, R. 1977, Foreign language teaching and bilingual education: Implications of some recent research findings. Paper presented to the ACTFL Annual Conference, San Francisco, CA.

Program on Teaching Effectiveness 1976, A factorially designed experiment on teacher structuring, soliciting and reacting. (R & D Memorandum No. 147). Stanford, CA: Stanford Center for Research and Development in Teaching.

RAMIREZ, A. and STROMQUIST, N. 1979, ESL methodology and student language learning in bilingual elementary schools. *TESOL Quarterly* 13, 145–58.

RAMIREZ, J.D., MERINO, B. and YUEN, S.D. 1985, *Classroom Observation Measures: Classroom Engaged Academic Time Measure and Classroom Language Observation Measure*. Mountain View, CA: SRA Technologies, Inc.

RAMIREZ, J.D., YUEN, S.D., RAMEY, D.R. and MERINO, B. 1986, *First Year Report: Longitudinal Study of Immersion Programs for Language-Minority Children*. Mountain View, CA: SRA Technologies, Inc.

SCHINKE-LLANO, L. 1983, Foreigner talk in content classrooms. In H. SELIGER and M. LONG (eds), *Classroom Oriented Research in Second Language Acquisition*. Rowley, MA: Newbury House.

SHULTZ, J. 1975, Language use in bilingual classrooms. Paper presented at the Annual Convention of Teachers of English to Speakers of Other Languages (TESOL), Los Angeles, CA.

SWAIN, M. 1983, Communicative competence: Some roles of comprehensible input and comprehensible output in its development. Paper presented at the 10th University of Michigan Conference on Applied Linguistics, Ann Arbor, MI.

—— 1984, A review of immersion education in Canada: Research and evaluation studies. In *Studies on Immersion Education: A Collection for United States Educators*. Sacramento, CA: California State Department of Education.

TIKUNOFF, W. and VAZQUEZ-FARIA, J. 1982, Successful instruction for bilingual schooling. *Peabody Journal of Education* 59, 234–71.

TRUEBA, H. and WRIGHT, P. 1981, A challenge for ethnographic researchers in bilingual settings: analyzing Spanish-English classroom interaction. *Journal of Multilingual and Multicultural Development* 2, 243–57.

WAGGONER, D. 1981, Educational attainment of language minorities in the United States. *NABE Journal* 6, 41–53.

WILLIG, A. 1985, A meta-analysis of selected studies on the effectiveness of bilingual education. *Review of Educational Research* 55 (3), 269–317.

WONG FILLMORE, L., AMMON, P., AMMON, M., DELUCCHI, K., JENSEN, J., MCLAUGHLIN, B. and STRONG, M. 1983, Learning language through bilingual instruction: Second year report. Submitted to the National Institute of Education, Berkeley, CA: University of California.

WONG FILLMORE, L., AMMON, P., MCLAUGHLIN, B. and AMMON, M. 1985, Learning English through bilingual instruction. Final report submitted to the National Institute of Education, Berkeley, CA: University of California.

WONG FILLMORE, L. and VALADEZ, C. 1986, Teaching bilingual learners. In M.C. WITTROCK (ed.), *Handbook of Research on Teaching* (3rd ed). New York: Macmillan.

6 Instructional discourse in 'effective' Hispanic classrooms[1]

EUGENE E. GARCIA

Introduction

The study of instruction continues to unfold increasing complexities in theories of linguistics, learning, cognition and socialization. What was once a study of learning has become today an interactive study of linguistic, psychological and social domains, each important in its own right, but together converging in broader attempts to construct and reconstruct the nature of instruction. These converging perspectives acknowledge the multifaceted nature of social interaction (Cazden, 1972; Hymes, 1974; Mehan, 1979; Garcia, 1983; and Marine-Dirshimer, 1985).

A primary issue in instruction of Hispanic children is understanding instructional interaction. Children from different linguistic cultures will use language in ways that reflect their different social environments. Interest in instructional discourse has generated studies in Hispanic bilingual mother–child, teacher–child and child–child interaction. Garcia (1983) reports an investigation of mother–child interaction including the description of Spanish/English use by children and caregivers in three different contexts: (3) pre-school instruction periods; (2) pre-school freeplay periods; and (1) the home. These descriptions pointed out very consistently that children, in particular, were 'choosing' to initiate a discourse in either Spanish or English as a function of the language which the mother was using to initiate discourse. A close qualitative examination of these same mothers and children interacting is reported by Garcia & Carrasco (1981). This analysis suggested that almost 90% of mother–child interactions were initiated by the mother, most often in Spanish. That is, mothers most often did not allow children to initiate discourse. For those small number of discourse instances in which children did initiate discourse, the topic determined language choice. That is 'what' the child spoke about was highly correlated with the language he/she chose to speak.

The richest data with regard to child topic initiation comes from child–child interactions. Ginishi (1981) while investigating the use of Spanish and English among first-graders concluded that the general language initiate rule for these students was: 'Speak to the listener in his/her best language'. Her analysis suggests that children when speaking with other children first made an unconscious choice regarding language of initiation based on their previous language use history with their fellow students. Zentella (1981) agrees that bilingual students do make these decisions. However, she found another discourse rule operating: 'you can speak to me in either Spanish or English.' Although Ginishi's (1981) and Zentella's (1981) discourse rules differ, each observation suggests that bilingual students make use of their social and language use history to construct guidelines related to discourse initiation. These studies suggest that particular sociolinguistic environments lead bilingual students to be aware of language choice issues related to discourse initiation.

A comprehensive understanding of early childhood bilingualism must, therefore, take into consideration more than the linguistic nature of the bilingual or the child's cognitive attributes. It must consider the child's surrounding environment. Recent data tentatively suggests that social context will determine:

1. The specific linguistic and meta-linguistic information important for the development of each language;
2. The specific social language use rules for each language;
3. The roles assigned to each language (Garcia, 1986).

Given the importance of social context for understanding the development of bilingualism in children, it is instructive to note that few recent studies in bilingual education adequately address this issue. Survey work by Halcon (1981) and Development Associates (1984) provide some general patterns of language-minority instructional discourse patterns in the United States. Tikunoff (1983) provides some descriptive information regarding instructional discourse patterns in bilingual programs. And a more intensive study by Wong Fillmore et al. (1985) provides a more focused picture of specific language use attributes and their effects on oral language development of language minority students.

Halcon (1981) sampled some 224 schools throughout the United States that had received three to five years of federal support for the education of language-minority students (under Basic Grants, Title VII, ESEA). English was the language most widely used in these bilingual programs. It was used more frequently than the native language in the typical classroom.

In contrast to Halcon's study of only federal programs serving language-minority students, Development Associates (1984) reports sampling 335 schools in 191 public school districts representing 19 states that were serving language-minority students (K–grade 5) regardless of funding sources for such programs. The number of schools selected in each state was determined by using a probability sampling formula that took into account the proportion of language-minority students in the state. Use of this sampling technique allowed the study to make broader generalizations (weighted estimates) regarding the character of instruction available to language-minority students in the United States. This study utilized both the data of the local school district and its own definition of language-minority students.

For those schools sampled by Development Associates (1984), the following results were found: (1) Eight separate treatments regarding the use of the native/home language were identified, ranging from only the use of native/home language to the total nonuse of the native/home language. (2) 93% of the schools sampled reported that use of English was the key ingredient in their programs; conversely, 7% indicated that use of the native/home language was the key ingredient. (3) 60% of the sampled schools reported that both the native/home language and English were used during instruction. (4) 30% of the sampled schools reported minimal use of the home/native language; only 3% reported use of English only. The majority (90%) of schools in this study reported the use of both the native/home language and English during instruction. A majority (30%) of these schools used the native/home language substantially, whereas a significant minority (50%) used it to a lesser degree. Regardless of the reported use of the native/home language, a clear majority (93%) of these schools reported that the use of English dominated instructional programs.

Tikunoff (1983) in the report of the Significant Bilingual Instructional Features Study (SBIF) also addressed the issue of language use in language minority classrooms. The 58 classrooms observed in this study were located in six school sites throughout the United States, and they included a variety of non-English languages. All classrooms in the study were considered effective on two criteria: (1) they were nominated by members of four constituencies—teachers, other school personnel, students, and parents; (2) teachers were found to produce rates of academic learning time—a measure of student engagement on academic tasks—as high as or higher than those reported in other research on effective teaching.

Instructional features found to be unique to language-minority student education included the use of two languages, special activities for teaching a second language, and instructional practices that took advantage of students' cultural background. According to the SBIF report, English was used approximately 60% of the time, and either the student's native language or a combination of the native language and English was used the rest of the time, with the percentage of English increasing with grade level. An additional significant instructional feature was the particular way in which the two languages were combined. Teachers of LEP students mediated instruction for LEP students by using the students' native language and English for instruction, alternating between the two languages whenever necessary to ensure clarity of instruction. Moreover, Tikunoff (1983) reports that students learned the language of instruction when engaged in instructional tasks expressed in that language. This integrative approach to developing English-language skills during ongoing instruction in the regular classroom contrasts with the more traditional, pull-out procedures, in which LEP students leave the regular instructional setting to receive ESL instruction.

Wong Fillmore et al. (1985) provide a detailed analysis regarding the influence of classroom practices on the development of oral English in Hispanic- and Chinese-background language-minority students. In this study, 17 Hispanic and Chinese-language-minority student classrooms (13 third grade and 4 fourth grade) served as sites. These students were in classrooms in which the native language and English were used during instruction, or, used only English during instruction. Specific measures of English-language production and comprehension were obtained over an academic-year period. In addition, classroom observations documented the character of teacher–student and student–student interaction as well as the organizational features of instruction. These authors reported a series of potentially significant observations:

1. Instructional practices that were related to English-language development were dependent on the student's initial level of English proficiency. Therefore, instructional practices such as high levels of teacher and peer interaction were more highly related to enhanced English development for nonproficient speakers of English.
2. The instructional variables that were related to enhanced English-language development were different for Hispanic versus Chinese-background students. Chinese-background students seemed to do best under classroom conditions in which they received independent help on English-language learning and in classrooms in which the instructional style was characterized by teacher-directed instruction.

Hispanic-background students demonstrated enhanced oral English-language development under classroom conditions in which there were more opportunities to interact with English-speaking peers.

In addition, these researchers report that growth in English-language production and comprehension was related to several attributes of student–teacher interaction. Classrooms in which teachers adjusted the language level of their interaction based on student feedback were more likely to produce overall English-language gains. Allowing and encouraging student participation and calling attention to the structure of language while using it were characterized as features which also enhanced language development.

These studies strongly suggest that teachers can play a significant role in English-language development for language-minority students. Finally, the research identifies the importance of peer interaction during English-language acquisition and the influence of initial English-language proficiency levels. It is this particular finding which served as a basis of the present research.

Present research

Specifically, the study presented in this chapter builds on this previous research and provides an analysis of a set of audio-video recorded, teacher–student and student–student interactions in a highly selective kindergarten, third grade and fifth grade classrooms identified for study because of their academic success with Hispanic students. Specifically, the study sought to identify what aspects of these interactions were similar to previous conceptual treatments of interaction during formal 'instruction time' (lessons) at micro-interactional levels (Mehan, 1979). The analysis used in this study is based on the notion that teaching is a fundamental act of two-way interaction between teacher and students (Garcia & Carrasco, 1981).

In performing the empirical assessment of teacher–student interaction, this study relied upon the Mehan interactional analysis model, for analyzing the sequential organization of speech acts within classroom lessons. This model concentrates on the sequential characteristics of teacher initiations, followed by student responses, and teacher evaluations. In so doing, this form of interaction analysis takes into consideration both the teacher and student utterances, topic selection, and conversational management in turn taking. It was hypothesized that the original Mehan model of instructional interaction sequencing would assist in describing the similarities and differences for the present teacher–student interactions. However, some modification of the Mehan model was necessary to accommodate the conversational data that were actually encountered (see Table 1).

As indicated earlier the present analysis is based on results reported by Mehan (1979) regarding elementary teaching styles. Specifically, Mehan found that elementary teachers when 'giving a lesson' tend to:

1. Begin a topic-oriented instructional exchange between themselves and their students by an elicitation statement (for example, 'What color is this block?'). Mehan had divided these elicitation statements into four categories that depended on the cognitive complexity of the intended response: (1) choice; (2) product; (3) process; and (4) meta-process. (See Table 1 for specific definitions and examples.) At times, teachers also use directives ('point to the red block.') or informatives ('This is a block.') in their lessons. These are used less often and are not intended to elicit a student response.
2. Terminate topic-oriented instructional exchanges between themselves and their students with an evaluation statement, such as, 'that was excellent'. Table 1 presents specific categories of such teacher replies.

How do students 'perform' during their lessons? Mehan (1979) reports that in response to the topic-oriented teacher elicitations, students tend most often to reply in accordance with the teacher's elicitation. However, they may also (1) not reply, (2) attempt to change the discourse topic, (3) react in a negative manner, (4) repeat the previous teacher statement, or, (5) indicate non-understanding of the teacher statement. Table 1 details possible replies.

Mehan describes the 'total' lesson discourse with the following interaction model:

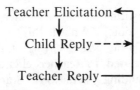

Most formal lessons follow the solid lines of diagrammed model: teacher elicits, students reply, and teacher replies. However, the dotted line indicates that at times the instruction is cut short when the teacher does not reply.

Using the above analytical scheme, the purpose of the present analysis was to assess the instructional style of the 'effective' teachers of Hispanic

TABLE 1 *Definition of interactional characteristics during instruction*

I. *Teacher initiations*
   A. Elicitations
      1. Choice: An elicitation act in which the initiator provides responses in elicitation itself. ('Is it blue or green?')
      2. Product: An elicitation act to which the respondent is to provide a factual response. ('What is this?')
      3. Process: An elicitation act which asks the respondent for opinions and interpretations. ('What's he doing?')
      4. Meta-process: An elicitation act which asks the respondent to be reflective on the process of reasoning itself. ('Why does he?')
   B. Directives: These are preparatory exchanges designed to have respondents take specific actions. ('Look here.')
   C. Informatives: Acts which pass on information, facts, opinions, or ideas. ('This girl's dress is blue.')

II. *Student reply*
   A. No reply: Student does not answer initiation acts, silence for a 2-second period.
   B. Topic-relevant reply
      1. Choice: Choice response relevant to the initiator's topic. ('Blue.')
      2. Product: Product response relevant to the initiator's topic. ('Car.')
      3. Process: Process response relevant to the initiator's topic. ('Playing with a dog.')
      4. Meta-process: Meta-process response relevant to the initator's topic. ('Cause he's not scared.')
   C. Bid: These constitute statements which attempt to gain the floor, i.e. change the topic. ('What is this?')
   D. Initiation: Initiating statement by the student which is topic-relevant: (1) related to teacher elicitation, (2) without teacher elicitation—'standing elicitation'. Standing elicitation: may (a) invite response or (b) be a comment only.
   E. Reaction: Negative acts taken in response to a directive. ('I don't want to.')
   F. Repetition: Student repeats the previous teacher/child statements.
   G. Don't understand: Student indicates that he did not understand initiator. ('What?')

TABLE 1 *Continued*

III. *Teacher reply*
   A. Repetition: Teacher repeats previous child utterance: (1) partially, (2) exactly, (3) expanded.
   B. Evaluation: Teacher (1) accepts (positive) or (2) rejects (negative) previous student utterance. ('O.K., that's good': 'not that way.')
   C. Prompts: Statements given in response to incorrect, incomplete or misunderstood replies. ('There are three.')
   D. Student topic initiator: Initiating statements in response to initiations or bids by the student. ('There are two tigers.')

students. Specifically the following questions were asked:

1. What type of instruction style does the teacher utilize when formally fulfilling the role of classroom instruction?
2. Does the instructional style of these 'successful' teachers differ from that reported for teachers with the same student population?
3. Does the instructional style differ in the incorporation of L1 and L2?

Selection of classrooms

The classrooms selected to participate in the study were chosen from kindergarten, third grade and fifth grade classrooms nominated by school district administrative and teaching personnel in 12 metropolitan Phoenix school districts. Specific selection of classrooms which would participate in the study was dependent on:

A. Consistent nomination and high ratings by nominators.
B. Evaluation of academic achievement (standardized test results for the past 2 years) indicating that the Hispanic classroom participants were at or above grade level.

Therefore, the classrooms chosen for this investigation were recognized in the local metropolitan area as 'excellent' classrooms for Hispanics and demonstrated academic achievement on standardized measures.

Methods of data collection

The teachers and students were audio-video recorded for purposes of instructional discourse analysis. The teachers were scheduled for audio-video tape recordings during small group lessons once every month for a total period of 5 months. The teachers were recorded for a period of 15–20 minutes during literacy (reading) instruction. This entailed the teacher interacting with 3–5 students for a period of 15–30 minutes. The camera was set 10–15 feet from the lesson site and was held stable on a tripod.

Results

Instructional discourse

Table 2 presents the percentage of (1) teacher initiations, (2) child replies and (3) teacher replies during audio-video recorded lessons for Spanish and English in the kindergarten, third grade and fifth grade classrooms studied. Teacher initiation statements at kindergarten and third grade tended to be dominated by directives and informatives (64.5% and 51.5%, respectively), and, choice and product elicitations (30% and 31%, respectively). Relatively few process (0% and 15.5%) and even less meta-process (1%–2%) type elicitations were observed. For fifth grade, less directives and informatives were observed (28%) along with more choice (20%), product (24%) and process (26%) elicitations.

Child replies during these interactions were dominated by child initiations, nearly 50% for all grade levels. This finding is most interesting since it reflects a high degree of student–student interaction which was topic related. Teacher replies consisted primarily of repetitions (17%, 27.5%, and 44%, respectively for kindergarten, third grade and fifth grade) and positive evaluative remarks (11%, 28.5% and 46%, respectively). Child topic initiations were relatively high (25%) for only third grade.

Recall that the typical teacher–student lesson discourse style as reported by Mehan (1979) might best be diagrammed as indicated in 'A' in Figure 1 below with a heavy weight on product and process type interaction. However, the student dominated interactional style observed (at all grade levels) is best characterized by 'B' in Figure 1 below.

Although teacher initiations were not of the process or meta-process type (except at grade 5), and, therefore similar to other reported findings of teacher–student interaction, the children played an important role in the discussion. That is, the interactions begun by teachers involved a high degree of student-to-student interaction, a large percentage of these inviting fellow student comment regarding the instructional topic.

TABLE 2 *Percentage of Spanish and English teacher initiation, child reply, and teacher reply for kindergarten, third grade and fifth grade during small group instruction*

Teacher initiation

	Choice		Product		Process		Meta-process		Directives		Informatives	
	S	E	S	E	S	E	S	E	S	E	S	E
Kind.	13%	0	17	0	0	0	5.5	0	42.5	0	22	0
Third	5.5	0	20	5.5	5.5	10	0	1	17	15	5.5	14
Fifth	0	20	0	24	0	26	0	2	0	14	0	14

Child reply

	Choice		Product		Process		Meta-process		Bid		Child Initiations	
	S	E	S	E	S	E	S	E	S	E	S	E
Kind.	2%	0	18	1	1	0	1	0	13	0	61	3
Third	3	1	32	4	4	6	0	1	3	3	26	17
Fifth	0	4	0	15	0	32	0	2	0	0	0	47

Teacher reply

	Repetition		Evaluation		Prompt		Child topic initiations	
	S	E	S	E	S	E	S	E
Kind.	17	0	11	0	6	0	6.6	0
Third	23	14.5	17	9.5	8	1.5	14	11
Fifth	0	44	0	46	0	3	0	7

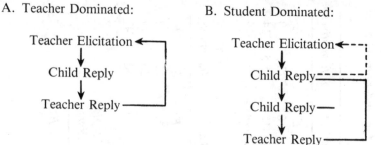

FIGURE 1   *Lesson discourse styles*

Language use

Table 2 provides a picture of actual language use during instruction. For kindergarten, almost all teacher and child initiations and replies were in Spanish. In fact, no teacher initiatives or replies were observed in English. The majority (3%) of these replies in English served only to open discussion with other students. Therefore in kindergarten, the language used was primarily Spanish, although some English was observed in student-to-student discourse. For third grade, both languages were used by teachers and students. The teachers split language use almost in half during discourse initiations (56.5% for Spanish, 44.5% for English). During their replies, students' interactions were primarily in Spanish (68%) although English was also observed. Teachers' replies were also primarily in Spanish (62%), however, English replies were at significant levels (38%).

For fifth grade, all teacher and student discourse was in English. No interaction, even among the students was observed in Spanish. Keeping in mind that these data are not longitudinal, but instead cross-sectional, it appears that *Spanish* is clearly the language of both teachers and students at kindergarten, *Spanish and English* serve as instructional languages at third grade, and, *English* significantly dominates over Spanish at fifth grade.

Discussion

The present study examined instructional interaction under conditions which were identified as academically successful. Previous research with ethnolinguistic students has suggested a potential mismatch between the culture of the home and that of the school (Ramirez & Castaneda, 1974). Similarly, research has suggested potential discrepancies in specific interactional styles (Ramirez & Castaneda, 1974; Zentella, 1981). Results of the present study extend these previous findings to 'effective' Hispanic classrooms.

In the present study's analysis of instructional styles, observation of 'effective' kindergarten, third grade and fifth grade teachers of 'successful' Hispanic (bilingual and non-bilingual) students indicated:

1. Teachers tended to provide an instructional initiation often reported in the literature. They elicited student responses but did so at relatively lower order cognitive and linguistic levels (except for fifth grade).
2. However, once a lesson elicitation occurred, students were allowed to take control of the specific lesson topic and were able to do so along with inviting fellow student interaction.

Significant was the finding that the teacher was clearly allowing student-to-student interaction in the child reply component of the instructional discourse segment. That is, the teacher was much more inviting of a student's 'call' for general student participation once the instructional interaction was set in motion. This finding is particularly important from linguistic and academic perspectives. Garcia (1983) has suggested that such student-to-student interaction discourse strategies are important in enhanced linguistic development. Wong Fillmore *et al.* (1985) report a similar finding for Hispanic children. Moreover, McClintock, Bayard & McClintock (1983) and Kagan (1983) have suggested that schooling practices which focus on cooperative child–child instructional strategies are in line with social motives in some Mexican American families. The 'style' documented here is in line with the 'style' documented as linguistically and culturally of benefit to Mexican American students.

The use of Spanish and English during instructional discourse shifted from an emphasis in Spanish at kindergarten, to the substantive use of Spanish and English in third grade, to the total use of English by fifth grade. This shift in Spanish to English use was observed for both teachers and students. Keep in mind that these classrooms were made up of children who were to some extent Spanish/English bilinguals, although this description is not as accurate for kindergarten as for third graders and fifth graders. Recall also that these children were in academically successful classrooms and the students themselves were reported to be at or above grade level on standardized achievement measure and identified as 'academically successful' by their teachers. These classrooms, with respect to language use, conform closely to earlier discussed reports by Halcon (1981), Development Associates (1984) and Wong Fillmore & Valadez (1985). That is, the native language may be used initially at early grade levels in language minority classrooms, but by later grade levels (in this case, fifth grade) English becomes the key language for instructional discourse.

The present study addressed aspects of previous work related to the instructional discourse and language use in language minority instructional settings. It did so by a micro-analysis of instructional style between a teacher and students in highly successful schooling contexts. However, the study also extends that previous work. In particular, teacher lesson interaction with students was not found to differ at the first 'elicitation' phase of instructional discourse. However, teachers in these successful classrooms were more willing to enhance interaction by setting the occasion for significant student-to-student interaction during small group lessons. These interactions shifted from predominantly Spanish in kindergarten to predominantly English in fifth grade.

Further research of this type would do much to delineate the particular components of the successful and not-so-successful instructional discourse. These types of analyses are of particular significance to Hispanic students whose academic future seems critically related to the nature and success of instructional communication.

Note to Chapter 6

1. This work was supported in major part by a grant from the Inter-University Program for Latino Research and the Social Science Research Council.

References

CADZEN, C. 1972, *Child Language and Education*. New York: Holt, Rinehart and Winston.

Development Associates, 1984, *Final Report: Descriptive Study Phase of the National Longitudinal Evaluation of the Effectiveness of Service for Language Minority Students*. Arlington, VA: Development Associates.

GARCIA, E. 1983, *Bilingualism in Early Childhood*. Albuquerque, New Mexico: University of New Mexico Press.

—— 1986, Bilingual development and the education of bilingual children during early childhood. *American Journal of Education* 95, (1), 96–121.

GARCIA, E. and CARRASCO 1981, An analysis of bilingual mother–child discourse. In R. DURAN (ed.), *Latino Discourse* pp. 173–89. New York: Ablex Publications.

GINISHI, C. 1981, Codeswitching in Chicano six-year-olds. In R. DURAN (ed.), *Latino Language and Communication Behavior* pp. 133–52. Norwood, NJ: Ablex Publishing Corporation.

HALCON, J. 1981, Features of Federal bilingual program. *NABE Journal* 6, 1, 27–39.

HYMES, D. 1974, *Foundation in Sociolinguistics: An Ethnographic Approach*. Philadelphia: University of Pennsylvania Press.

KAGAN, S. 1983, Social orientation among Mexican–American children: A challenge to traditional classroom structures. In E. GARCIA (ed.), *The Mexican American Child*. pp. 163–182. Tempe, AZ: Arizona State University.

McCLINTOCK, E., BAYARD, M. and McCLINTOCK, C. 1983, The socialization of social motives in Mexican–American families. In E. GARICA (ed.), *The Mexican American Child* pp. 143–162. Tempe, AZ: Arizona State University.

MEHAN, H. 1979, *Learning Lessons*. Cambridge, Mass.: Harvard University Press.

MARINE-DIRSHIMER, G. 1985, *Talking, Listening and Learning in Elementary Classrooms*. New York: Longman.

RAMIREZ, M. and CASTANEDA, A. 1974, *Cultural Democracy, Bicognitive Development and Education*. New York: Academic Press.

TIKUNOFF, W.J. 1983, *Significant Bilingual Instructional Features Study*. San Francisco, CA: Far West Laboratory.

WONG FILLMORE, L., AMMON, M.S. and McLAUGHLIN, B. 1985, Learning English through bilingual instruction. NIE Final Report #400–360–0030. Rosslyn, VA: National Clearinghouse for Bilingual Education.

WONG FILLMORE, L. and VALADEZ, C. 1985, Teaching bilingual learners. In M.C. WITTROCK (ed.), *Handbook on Research on Teaching*. Washington, DC: AERA.

ZENTELLA, A.C. 1981, Ta bien, You could answer me en cualquier idioma: Puerto Rican codeswitching in bilingual classroom. In R. DURAN (ed.), *Latino Language and Communicative Behavior* pp. 109–132. Norwood, NJ: Ablex Publishing Corporation.

Section III
Technological Advances

7 Bilingual interactive video: Let the student switch languages[1]

RAYMOND V. PADILLA

Several years ago Gustavo Gonzalez and Lento Maez (1980) wrote an article titled 'To Switch or Not to Switch: The Role of Code-Switching in the Elementary Bilingual Classroom'. With such mock melodrama they entered into a serious discussion of an issue that has important implications for bilingual education practice: Should the two languages typically used in bilingual instruction be strictly separated or can they be used in alternating fashion without adversely affecting the learning process? The common wisdom in the field generally holds that the two languages should be equal but separate. A few individuals have argued that the two languages can be used concurrently as long as carefully specified procedures are followed. This article reports on the potential use of interactive video technology in the context of language distribution issues in bilingual instruction.

The issue of language distribution

The use of two languages as media of instruction immediately raises the issue of how and when each language is to be used. One also needs to determine how much and for how long each language is to be used across the breadth and length of the curriculum. In addition, it is important to determine whether the two languages will be used separately (for example, in different classrooms, or class periods) or concurrently (through such devices as immediate translation or the mixing of the two languages). Intuitively, it would seem that different decisions on these issues could possibly lead to differences in educational outcomes, and certainly they will lead to important differences in the management of instructional resources.

Going beyond intuition, some researchers have tried to demonstrate the efficacy of a particular approach, for example, the New Concurrent Approach (Jacobson, 1981). However, it seems that more research will have to be done before the distributional issues can be decided on the basis of research evidence.

The language distribution issue tends to be colored by factors that properly speaking are not educational but have to do with everyday language behavior and the attitudes that people express toward such behavior. For example, it is not uncommon for individuals who speak two languages to mix the two languages together in some fashion during ordinary discourse. Often labeled as 'code switching', this behavior has been defined by Gonzalez & Maez (1980: 126) as '... the alternating use of two or more languages during social interaction ... which may occur between utterances (*inter*sententially) or within utterance boundaries (*intra*-sententially)'. Since such language behavior can occur as early as elementary school, and even earlier, pedagogical questions naturally arise as to whether or not code switching is appropriate, and what use, if any, it might have in the methodology of teaching.

The predominant view seems to be that intra-sentential code switching (mixing languages within a sentence) does not have much positive value from a pedagogical point of view. When inter-sentential code switching (mixing languages between sentences) occurs without a specific pedagogical aim, it is also considered of little value by many educators. However, when inter-sentential code switching is utilized to achieve a specific pedagogic objective, then some authors consider such language behavior to be of potential value. Most prominent among these authors is Rodolfo Jacobson who has carefully developed the New Concurrent Approach.

Briefly, Jacobson advocates the concurrent use of two languages only for content instruction, leaving instruction about a language to be taught in the language itself. The alternation from one language (L1) to the other (L2) must occur smoothly and aim at conceptual and lexical reinforcement. Mere translation must be avoided, and the continuity of a lesson must be maintained across the language shifts. In short, the language shifts should be transparent to the learner as she/he focuses on the content that is to be learned.

To achieve such transparency, Jacobson developed a system of cues that should trigger acceptable language switches by the teacher. In summary, the system of cues is based on classroom strategies, the curriculum, language development, and interpersonal relations. Classroom strategies have to do with conceptual reinforcement, material review, capturing of attention, and teacher praise and reprimand. Curriculum cues are related to language appropriateness, topic, and text. Language development involves cues linked to variable language dominance, lexical enrichment, and translatability. Finally, cues related to interpersonal relationships have to do with social considerations such as intimacy/formality, courtesy, free choice, fatigue, self-awareness, and rapport. For a detailed discussion of the New Concurrent Approach see Jacobson (1981).

As might be expected, the complexity of such a system of cues necessitates a fairly high level of environmental monitoring, as well as self monitoring, by the teacher. With appropriate training and very solid control of the two languages, some teachers can undoubtedly become proficient in this monitoring behavior. Others, particularly those less proficient in L2, may well have difficulty achieving a high enough level of transparency as they attempt to switch from one language to the other as prescribed by the New Concurrent Approach.

The entire system of cues assumes teacher reaction to student language behavior, rather than the other way around. The idea is to maximize communication between teacher and student by having the teacher adjust to the linguistic needs of each child and the class as a whole. In an ordinary classroom situation, this is probably the only reasonable way to maximize communication given the unpredictable nature of the students' language performance. But what if the students were able to decide when to switch languages? What if they were in control of the language of instruction?

The interactive video approach

Student control of the instructional language is possible if interactive video technology is used. Interactive video combines several technologies—microcomputers, video production, and instructional design—to create a highly individualized system of instruction that maximizes the audio/visual impact of video players and the logical functions of a computer. When applied to bilingual instruction, interactive video can make language switching truly transparent as the student selects the language of instruction from one instructional segment to another. The computer is able to provide instruction in either L1 or L2 or any combination of the two (within the limits programmed in the computer). As a result, one student can complete the entire curriculum in L1; another student may complete the entire curriculum in L2; and still another student may complete it in both L1 and L2 in whatever proportion of the two languages the student desires. In short, instruction through interactive video permits the student to select between monolingual instruction in either language or bilingual instruction as the student needs it.

A typical interactive video system includes a microcomputer, a video cassette player (or video disk player), hardware to connect the two components together, and software both to run the system and to present the instructional material (for a more detailed discussion see Miller, 1987). In addition, a curriculum must be designed in pursuit of stated goals and objectives and with appropriate procedures to assess student learning (Dean & Whitlock, 1983). If the required audio and visual material is not an off-the-shelf product, it must be produced locally. This could be a costly proposition and should be considered carefully before any commitments are made. For background information on interactive video see Floyd & Floyd (1982), Iuppa (1984), and Kinderberger (1984).

The equipment used in the pilot project reported here included the following components:

1. IBM PC with 256 K of random access memory.
2. Sony K11-HG color monitor capable of receiving both an RGB signal from the computer and a composite signal from the VCR.
3. Video Cassette Recorder (Panasonic NV-8200).
4. A Whitney interactive video control box.
5. Whitney authoring system to develop and deliver the lessons.

To create a proper development environment, supplementary components were added to this basic system, including a printer, a BASIC interpreter, and a word processor.

Since the project was implemented on a modest budget, the development team was made up largely of graduate students. With the exception of the author and another staff researcher, the project team consisted of graduate students in bilingual education, educational technology, and computer engineering. Voice talent and technical video production skills were provided by other graduate students. An advisory committee composed of individuals from academia, industry, and the Arizona Department of Education provided criticism and assistance to the technical team.

The general instructional goal was to develop a bilingual interactive video curriculum in English and Spanish for the purpose of training an individual, who might be limited English proficient, to use and operate an IBM PC at a beginner's level of proficiency. The assumptions made about the intended learner were as follows:

1. The learner was assumed to have a minimum general language

proficiency in either English or Spanish at the level expected of someone who has completed successfully the tenth grade.

2. The learner was not expected to have prior experience with micro-computers.

On the basis of these assumptions, a curriculum was prepared that focused on learning how to operate a PC at the beginner's level. The lessons developed focused on nomenclature, the basic functions of a micro-computer, component interconnection, and internal and external DOS commands. All video segments were produced locally. Native speakers were used for both English and Spanish. The project required close collaboration between curriculum developers, bilingual education specialists, video production crew, and computer programmers. The entire project was completed in two years.

In a typical learning session, the student sits in front of the computer and operates the keyboard. The monitor is at a comfortable height and distance so that the student can easily read text material and observe images on the screen. For the first time user, the instructor shows the student how to enter a command and tell the computer to execute it by pressing the ENTER key.

Once the program is loaded and running, the student reads and hears a welcome message followed by top level menus that allow the student to select the initial language of instruction and the specific unit of a lesson that a student wishes to study. After the student views a small segment of instruction, the computer asks a series of questions to determine if the student has learned the material presented. If the student fails to answer a question correctly, the computer will repeat the relevant audio/visual segment and retests the student. At the end of the lesson, the student has the option to repeat the lesson in either of the two languages or to continue with the next lesson, again in either of the two languages.

Results of the field test

Once the bilingual interactive video curriculum was completed, a field trial was conducted using students from a local community college. Because of the location of the college, some of the students had received part of their public school education in Mexico; many were enrolled in a special Vocational English as a Second Language (VESL) program in the college.

A total of fifteen students participated in the pilot study. They ranged in age from 22 to 69. Most had been identified previously (by the host community college) as limited English proficient. This determination was made on the basis of program eligibility criteria for a federally funded Vocational English as a Second Language (VESL) project. A key eligibility criterion was that the students had not been able to matriculate as regular community college students because they did not possess sufficient proficiency in English to be able to attend regular classes. Also, all students participating in the field trial were asked to rate their proficiency in English and Spanish. These self-ratings are summarized in Table 1. Seven of the participants were born and/or had some education outside of the U.S., mostly in Mexico. The majority of the students (eight of the fifteen) had no prior experience with computers and the remaining portion had less than one year of experience.

Each student was allowed to take an interactive video lesson individually. When the lesson was completed, the student was asked to complete a questionnaire dealing with language and educational background as well as experience with computers. Initially, the student was instructed on the use and location of the return key (necessary to enter commands) and the backspace key (necessary for making corrections when entering commands). The average time for the interactive video session was 25 minutes, with a range of 15 to 42 minutes (see Table 2).

Following the initial screen display, which contains acknowledgements and other notices, the student was presented with the highest level menu. This menu gives the student the option to select the language of instruction for the unit which is to follow. The language choice is between English and Spanish. Fifty-five percent of the students selected Spanish as the initial language of instruction. (Incidentally, the menu is presented in both English and Spanish, both in writing on the screen and orally through the video cassette recorder.) When asked why they selected Spanish as the initial language, the students generally reported that they felt most comfortable, confident, and proficient in that language.

TABLE 1 *Summary of self-ratings in English and Spanish language proficiency*

Language	Average self-rating*	Range	N
English	3.33	1–5	12
Spanish	4.07	2–5	14

* One is lowest and 5 is highest proficiency.

TABLE 2 *Summary of interactive video session field trial**

Item	Range	Average
Session time	15 to 42 min.	25.4 min
Units completed	1 to 4 units	2.5 units
Percent of questions answered correctly after first try	25 to 100	80.27

* Number of subjects = 15.

The bilingual interactive video system allows the student to switch languages at will. The only constraint is determined by the programmer who decides where to place the branching menu. In theory the branching (switching) menu can be made available as often as desired, but in practice computer resources must be managed wisely. If the student is allowed to switch after every sentence, for example, the lesson would have to be broken down into extremely small segments. This not only causes loss of instructional continuity, but is an extremely inefficient use of computer resources. A better choice is to allow the student to switch languages at the end of each unit or between lessons. Interactive video instructional units are quite short due to the limitations of many authoring systems. Yet they are long enough to maintain a coherent instructional sequence.

The options provided to the student at the end of each unit within a lesson, and at the end of each lesson, were as follows:

1. Repeat the current unit/lesson in the alternate language.
2. Repeat the current unit/lesson in the same language.
3. Proceed to the next unit/lesson in the same language.
4. Proceed to the next unit/lesson in the alternate language.

The student is thus able to control the level of redundancy in either a monolingual or bilingual mode. In addition, of course, the student controls the pacing of the instruction.

As already noted, slightly over half of the students decided to start the lesson in Spanish. Remarkably, of the fifteen subjects in the field trial only one made a language switch between units. For this group of students (many of whom were participating in a Vocational English as a Second Language project) the initial choice of language was crucial. The implication is that students of this type have a fairly accurate self assessment of the instructional language that is best for them. However, the instructional situation did not call for any oral language behavior by the students. They simply received information and pressed the appropriate key(s). It could be that more switches would occur if the students were required to actually produce oral language responses. Of course, the field trial could only monitor a relatively short period of instruction, and it is possible that the rate of language switching could be higher if a longer period of instruction were monitored.

The students were asked to rate the quality of the interactive video instruction on a number of variables. A Likert scale was used with choices ranging from 1 (worst) to 5 (best). Table 3 summarizes the student ratings on various aspects of the instruction.

As can be seen from Table 3, students like the presentation of visual and audio information, and they react well to the diagnostic assessment which is built into each small unit of instruction. They are generally satisfied with the overall system performance except for the wait that occurs while the video cassette recorder is shuttling to the next instructional segment. Interestingly, the idle time often is measured in seconds, and seldom exceeds

TABLE 3 *Student ratings of the interactive video instruction**

Item	Mean rating**
English voice	4.15
Spanish voice	4.33
Waiting time (machine shuttling)***	2.13
Machine response time***	3.87
Video presentation	4.27
Screen format	4.40
Appropriateness of questions (assessment of learning)	4.07
Screen colors	4.07
Pacing	3.67

* Number of students = 15.
** One is the lowest rating, five is the highest.
*** Shuttle time is the time that the VCR takes to find the proper tape segment.
Machine response time measures the speed with which the microcomputer executes instructions.

a minute or two. However, a few idle moments of real time in front of a monitor that appears to be doing nothing seems to equal a much longer wait in subjective time. Electronic media tend to create an intolerance for waiting; the user demands consistency in the responsiveness of the various components of the system—one component can not be appreciably slower than the others.

Some of the specific comments offered by the students indicate that they viewed the bilingual interactive video lesson as an opportunity for Spanish speakers to learn about computers in their own language while learning the technical English vocabulary necessary to work with computers in the future. They could listen to a voice in Spanish while they could see labels on the screen in English. They also felt that they were learning about computers 'hands-on'.

The students reported that the instruction was clear and very understandable. The assessment questions were very easy to understand and followed the information presented in the lesson segment. When a question was answered incorrectly, the relevant information was repeated ('If a person gets the wrong answer, it [the information] will be shown again.'). Along the same lines, they commented:

> 'The information and presentation allowed you to learn the lesson. I learned about the computer without thinking about it. Instructions were easy to follow.'

Conclusion

Language distribution issues have been an important topic in bilingual education ever since the first enactment of Title VII of the Elementary and Secondary Education Act. These issues are important because they reflect choices in language policy, in teaching methods, and in theories of learning. In general, the conventional pedagogic wisdom has been to keep the instructional languages separated. Some researchers, such as Rodolfo Jacobson and others, have argued the case for the controlled use of two languages concurrently. These researchers represent in an academic context the common sense knowledge of many teachers and bilingual individuals who are very much aware that two languages can be used concurrently in real life settings. They know that a coherent message can be communicated even when two languages are used to deliver it.

The methodology of the New Concurrent Approach is based on a fairly elaborate system of cues that must be understood and used by the teacher to select the immediate language of instruction. Learning this system requires training, practice, and a fairly high level of proficiency in both of the instructional languages. All of these elements are not always available to teachers during their preservice and inservice training. Moreover, the approach is largely teacher centered in the sense that the teacher decides when to legitimately switch languages. The student may switch languages but it is up to the teacher to determine how to legitimate the switch, if at all. In spite of these limitations, the New Concurrent Approach is a welcomed development for those teachers who do use two languages anyway, but who do not have a systematic way of doing it that takes into account important pedagogical considerations.

As reported in this article, interactive video technology offers a second way to implement concurrent language use in bilingual instruction. An important feature of this approach is that the student is in control of the language of instruction: The student can select monolingual instruction in L1 or L2 or bilingual instruction in whatever proportion of the two languages the student desires. In principle one could even use interactive video to implement mixed languages within an instructional segment. However, in the pilot study reported here the two languages were separated but made accessible in turn.

The results of the field trial indicate that students respond favorably to bilingual interactive video instruction. They were about evenly split between those who chose Spanish and those who chose English as the initial language of instruction. Surprisingly, perhaps, only one of the fifteen students elected to switch languages between instructional units. This is a provocative finding, but one that needs to be interpreted cautiously for the reasons already discussed; further study is certainly warranted to determine if this is typical language switching behavior for interactive video instruction.

Clearly, the work reported here has limitations, as does interactive video technology more generally. The pilot study focused on young adults and older students, many of whom were enrolled in a Vocational English as a Second Language program. It remains to be seen whether bilingual interactive video can be utilized effectively with younger students at the elementary and middle school levels. The scope of the project was limited to one content area (computer literacy). Other content areas need to be explored such as math, science, social studies, and language arts. The scope of the field trial was modest. Although the project lasted two years, the technical overhead was so high that the field trial had to be extremely modest in scope. Similar efforts are needed in other parts of the country and with different languages and populations before one can have confidence in the approach.

Finally, interactive video technology has important limitations. It is a very complex, convergent technology that relies on several technologies that are themselves complex: Computer hardware and software design, video production, curriculum design, learning assessment, etc. Adding bilingual features only complicates the situation further. Bilingual education specialists must be brought into the picture, individuals proficient in different languages must be employed, etc. Bilingual interactive video becomes an extremely complex technical activity that cannot be carried out by a single individual. All of this, of course, means that bilingual interactive video is not cheap. It is equipment intensive and expensive to program.

In spite of these and other limitations, the pilot study demonstrated that bilingual interactive video has many attractive features: It can be used effectively when expert knowledge is not readily available (such as fluency in non-English languages); it highly individualizes the rate of instruction; and it puts the student in control of instruction within the choices allowed by the program. Machines do not have prior expectations about how much a student can learn. They will go as fast and as far as the student wants to go. When they are programmed in more than one language, they will readily engage the student in any of the languages available. They are infinitely patient and will wait for the student indefinitely. They can push ahead or they can stand by patiently, and the student is always in control. They can easily let the student decide on the language of instruction. The question 'To switch or not to switch?' can be answered with one key stroke.

Note to Chapter 7

1. Members of the project team included Lento Maez, Martha Baca, Albert Gutierrez, and Vishnu Satya. The project reported in this article was supported by grants from the Arizona Department of Education. Their support is gratefully acknowledged, but the views expressed herein are not necessarily those of the funding agency.

References

DEAN, C. and WHITLOCK, Q. 1983, *A Handbook of Computer Based Training.* London: Nichols Publishing Company.
FLOYD, S. and FLOYD, B. 1982, *Handbook of Interactive Video.* White Plains, NY: Knowledge Industries Publications, Inc.

GONZALEZ, G. and MAEZ, L.F. 1980, To switch or not to switch: The role of code-switching in the elementary bilingual classroom. In R.V. PADILLA (ed.), *Theory in Bilingual Education* (*Ethnoperspectives in Bilingual Education Research, Vol. II*). Ypsilanti, MI: Eastern Michigan University.

IUPPA, N.V. 1984, *A Practical Guide to Interactive Video Design*. White Plains, NY: Knowledge Industries Publications, Inc.

JACOBSON, R. 1981, The implementation of a bilingual instruction model: The new concurrent approach. In R.V. PADILLA (ed.), *Bilingual Education Technology* (*Ethnoperspectives in Bilingual Education Research, Vol. III*). Ypsilanti, MI: Eastern Michigan University.

KINDERBERGER, C. 1984, *Interactive Video–1984*. St. Louis: Applied Video Technology.

MILLER, III, C.R. 1987, *Essential Guide to Interactive Videodisc Hardware and Applications*. Westport, CT: Meckler Publishing Corporation.

8 Second language use within the non-traditional classroom: Computers, cooperative learning, and bilingualism

ROBERT A. DeVILLAR

English, achievement and language minority students

English language proficiency and academic achievement are concepts that educators and researchers in the U.S. tend to interrelate (Cohen, 1986; De Avila *et al.*, 1983). The fundamental notion is that to succeed in school a child must at least know how to understand, speak, read, and write the language of the classroom. Language proficiency does not guarantee academic success, but its absence suggests poor academic achievement.[1] There are millions of school-age children, however, who are designated as lacking sufficient English language proficiency to be able to profit from instruction given solely in English. Oxford-Carpenter *et al.* (1984), for example, cite that 2.4 million school-age children are designated as Limited English Proficient (LEP), 75% of whom are Hispanic. Other sources (e.g. Stein, 1986: 172), cite the nationwide figure for LEP students as high as 3.6 million. Over the years, especially the past twenty, the educational needs of limited- and non-English speaking children have been addressed by school programs in different manners and to varying degrees. Three types of instructional setting, however, may be currently identified as major strategies of pedagogical intervention:

1. *Second language program setting.* A situation where the student's exposure to content area instruction in the second language (L2) is supplemented by formal L2 language learning instruction;

2. *Bilingual classroom setting.* A situation where the student's content area instruction is given, to varying degrees, in the student's native language (L1) and the second language (L2); and,

3. *Regular classroom setting.* A situation in which the student receives instruction in all content areas in the L2.

These intervention programs are neither mutually exclusive nor, given the many distinct programmatic types which exist within each major category, are they monolithic (Ramirez, 1985). The primary goal of each of these strategies, however, is identical: to convert non- and limited-English proficiency (NEP and LEP, respectively) students to fluent English speaking (FEP) students in order to significantly enhance the probability of their academic success within the U.S. school system.[2]

Irrespective of the type of instructional setting, however, the general outcome of these programs has not significantly improved the academic achievement or the English language proficiency of language minority children. This has been particularly conspicuous in the case of children whose first language is Spanish, where drop-out rates and retention rates have been higher, and degree of aspirations and expectations have been lower than any other minority group, except Native American and Hawaiian children (Hernandez-Chavez, 1984; Walker & Rakow, 1985). Furthermore, the problem, rather than diminishing in scale, is actually being compounded. From a demographics perspective, for example, the problem is exacerbated by the continuing large-scale immigration of mainly economically poor, non-English speaking families (Levin, 1985) and other related language minority population growth factors. In the case of Hispanics, for example, the differential growth rate between the total U.S. population (0.8% per annum) and that of the Hispanic U.S. population (2.2% per annum) is projected to be 1.4% per annum through the year 2000 (Oxford-Carpenter *et al.*, 1984).

Thus, the educational dilemma, which especially involves and affects Hispanic students, and which continues to perplex educators within the U.S., may be characterized by the following four factors:

1. a large and rapidly growing number of low-income children, who are seen as culturally different and whose first language is not English and accorded a low-status;

2. a persistent tradition of school failure and under achievement, especially in the areas of reading, vocabulary, and mathematics, coupled with immensely high drop-out rates;

3. a lack of English-language proficiency, both perceived and measured, which, in turn, justifies special instruction in English;

4. a trend to mainstream failing and underachieving minority group children into regular classrooms.

In summary, schools have experienced general and long-term failure in serving as a setting within which Hispanic and other language minority students learn English or significantly improve their education. Even within the special conditions of bilingual education and second language programs, generally inadequate research methods, especially non-randomization, have necessarily made suspect the validity of reported results (Willig, 1985). Also, bilingual programs continue to generally rely on federal funding rather than state or local funding, thereby limiting their educational reach, regardless of their utility value, to between 7 to 10% of the LEP population (Stein, 1986). Taking into account even these factors leaves little room for doubt that regular classroom instruction (also referred to as 'involuntary immersion'; see Ferguson & Heath, 1981: 35) continues as the predominant instructional strategy for most NEP and LEP students.

Researchers, therefore, continue to investigate factors, especially within the classroom experience, which promote or inhibit language development and use among children in general, and, more particularly, second language development and use among language minority children. Results of such research ultimately should affect the theoretical frameworks and methodologies employed in subsequent research efforts, as well as offer increasingly refined insights into the nature of a particular second-language related problem. The research reviewed below addresses second language opportunities within the three types of instructional settings previously described, providing evidence (1) that the settings are not conducive to attaining the language goals which they set, and (2) that second language opportunities are enhanced through cooperative-type grouping strategies complemented by enrichment-oriented computer-assisted instruction.

Language use within the regular classroom setting

In the traditional instructional setting, teachers dominate talk within the classroom (e.g. Flanders, 1970; Goodlad, 1986; Mehan, 1979). Within this setting, the amount of talk allocated per student would only average between 20 and 30 seconds, at best, per class period (Department of Education and Science, 1975; Goodlad, 1986; Long & Porter, 1985). The design and social structure of the traditional classroom also make it difficult for second language acquisition to co-occur with subject matter instruction. In this 'teacher-fronted, whole class' approach, the teacher generally stands at one end of the classroom with students, at individual desks, facing her.

Instruction by the teacher is given to the students according to a lesson plan designed to meet the needs of the class as a whole rather than to address the particular needs of a sub-group of students or otherwise diversify the instructional context. Finally, talk by students within this setting is predictable, consisting largely of short-answer responses to mainly factual questions for which the teacher already has the answer (Mehan, 1979).

Language use within the bilingual classroom setting

Even within a bilingual education setting, conditions for second language acquisition can be minimal. Milk (1980) identifies two reasons why second language acquisition can be constrained within this setting: (1) classroom grouping strategies (i.e. L1-dominant students in one group; L2-dominant students in another; balanced bilinguals in yet another) keep children of the same proficiency level together and thereby encourage use of dominant language as well as thwart exposure to, and meaningful communication in, the second language; and (2) teachers assume that second language acquisition will occur naturally within the bilingual classroom setting and therefore do not see a role for consciously planning its use and development.

Language use within the ESL setting

Learning a second language through special classroom instruction has seldom been a successful enterprise for students. Rubin (1975) describes the performance record of formal education in this area as:

> ...notoriously poor...no matter whether the success criterion is passing the course, acquiring certain skills (reading, writing, speaking and understanding) or actually putting to use what has been learned. (pp. 41–42).

A disadvantage generally characterizing the ESL classroom, and contributing to its performance record, is that it is designed along traditional instructional lines. Long & Sato (1983), for example, found that adult ESL classes offer very little opportunity for learners to practice the target language or to hear it used for communicative purposes. The limited amount of communicative language used is from the teacher, mainly in the form of imperatives relating to classroom management and disciplinary matters. Moreover, research since the 1950s has consistently demonstrated that no one language learning methodology significantly improves language learning outcomes more than any other (Richards & Rodgers, 1986). This concern for the significance of methodology in second language instruction relates to the more fundamental question regarding the extent to which a language can be taught (as opposed to learned). Knowledge of the language acquisition process together with the informed manipulation of that process for purposes of second language teaching are the two fundamental criteria upon which second language instruction is generally based. Given the present state of linguistic and language-learning knowledge, neither criterion can readily be satisfied nor necessarily assumed. Thus, at present, second language research maintains its focus primarily on the process of language acquisition, especially within regular classroom and non-school-related settings,where the process is occurring spontaneously within the learner (i.e. unassisted by 'systematic and intentional influence', see Klein, 1986: 18). And, due greatly to these research developments, more recent second language teaching approaches attempt to provide:

> opportunities for positive personal relationships to develop among learners and between learners and teacher. These relationships can help to 'humanize' the classroom and to create an environment that supports the individual in his efforts to learn. (Littlewood, 1986:18)

In summary, second language instruction on a formal basis, by itself, is not predicted to significantly improve the English language proficiency of language minority children.

Instructional trends: implications for second language use

Relatively recent research from the three areas of second language acquisition (e.g. Cummins, 1981: Enright & McCloskey, 1985 [review article]; Krashen, 1982), cooperative learning (e.g. Cohen, 1986; Johnson et al., 1984: Seeley, 1985; Slavin, 1983), and computer-assisted instruction (e.g. Becker, 1984/85; Hawkins, 1984; Johnson, Johnson & Stanne, 1985) have independently identified particular socio-psychological and contextual factors which appear to favorably influence language use and academic achievement within the instructional setting. The implications from this collective research challenge traditional models of instruction based mainly on whole-class instruction, competition-based learning, and teacher-centered learning. The respective alternatives which are offered as complementary strategies to the above include small-group instruction, cooperative-based learning, and peer-centered learning, each, or in combination, enhanced, with increasing regularity, by a computer-assisted instructional (CAI) setting.

The rationale for integrating alternative instructional practices with the more traditional ones is simple: the traditional instructional practices do not allow for qualitatively or quantitatively meaningful student verbal interaction within the class period (e.g. Mehan, 1979; Goodlad, 1986; Long & Porter, 1985), while the alternative instructional practices generally encourage and, whether by design or nature, produce it. Both cooperative learning and computer-assisted instructional settings, for example, have been found to facilitate talk among students (see, for example, Johnson *et al.*, 1984; Seeley, 1985; and Slavin, 1983, for reviews of cooperative learning research; see, for example, Becker, 1984/85 regarding the role of talk within computer-assisted instructional environment). And talk, as mentioned previously, is viewed as potentially leading to enhanced English language proficiency which is, in turn, associated with a heightened probability for successful achievement in school.

Cooperative learning, computers and language use

The trend toward cooperative learning is more than mere reaction to the traditional competitive model of learning. There is strong empirical evidence of its benefits from research in classrooms and laboratories. Benefits associated with cooperative learning are generally reported within the two broad categories of *non-cognitive* and *cognitive* (achievement) outcomes. Slavin (1983) reviewed non-cognitive outcomes of thirty cooperative learning research studies, applying as his selection criteria the following: (a) 'adequate methodological rigor', (b) practicality as an alternative to traditional instruction, and (c) cooperative learning methods that had been evaluated for at least two weeks within the elementary or secondary setting. Outcomes for students from cooperative learning settings were significantly different from those of student counterparts within competitive and individualistic settings in the following areas:

1. more cooperative and altruistic (i.e. giving more than receiving) behaviors;
2. greater mutual concern (e.g. liking for one another, feelings of being liked by others, number of perceived friends);
3. more positive race/ethnic relations within the classroom;
4. higher acceptance by 'normal progress' students of their 'low-achieving' mainstreamed peers;
5. greater liking of school;
6. higher self-esteem;
7. greater expression of norms favoring learning;

8. greater locus of control (i.e degree to which students feel that their outcomes depend on their own efforts).

Regarding cognitive outcomes, Johnson *et al.* (1981) conducted a meta-analysis of 122 studies carried out between 1924 and 1981 relative to social interdependence and achievement. They found that cooperative learning experiences generally promote higher achievement than do competitive and individualistic learning experiences irrespective of age or subject area. As the researchers point out:

> These results hold for all age levels, for all subject areas, and for tasks involving concept attainment, verbal problem-solving, categorization, spatial problem-solving, retention and memory, motor performance, and guessing-judging-predicting. (p. 15)

Johnson & Johnson's (1983) follow-up research to the Johnson *et al.* (1981) study identified factors contributing to the effectiveness of cooperative learning over its competitive and individualist model counterparts. The role and learning consequences of talk between students comprise the bulk of advantages associated with cooperative learning, as exemplified by the following:

1. discussion promoted discovery and development of higher quality cognitive strategies for learning, more so than within the competitive or individualistic learning situations;
2. participation produced conflict among the ideas, opinions, conclusions, theories, and information of the members, which promoted increased motivation to achieve, higher retention of the learned material, and greater depth of understanding;
3. discussion promoted (a) more frequent oral repetition of information, (b) stating of new information, and (c) explaining, integrating, and providing rationales, all of which promoted long-term retention of information and generally increased achievement;
4. peer regulation, feedback, support and encouragement was greater within a cooperative learning environment than within a competitive or individualistic one; and,
5. exchange of ideas among students from high, medium, and low achievement levels, and different ethnic backgrounds enriched their learning experiences, especially through accommodation to each other's perspectives. Higher achievers, moreover, within these groups never performed worse than their counterparts in competitive or individualistic learning settings. Also, when measured on related criteria (e.g. retention, quality of reasoning strategies),

higher achievers within cooperative learning settings scored higher than their above-mentioned counterparts.

Other research relating to cognitive benefits derived within mixed ability groupings (e.g. Peterson, Janicki & Swing, 1981) found that although students designated as higher ability gave more explanations than did their low ability partners, achievement of both giver and receiver of explanations was positively related to the giving of explanations (reported in Dickson & Vereen, 1983).

Relative to the cognitive advantages associated with cooperative learning within a computer-assisted instructional setting, Johnson, Johnson & Stanne (1985) found that (a) students who conducted their computer work in pairs or small groups, in which each participant had a definite role in the computing task, were found to produce more work which was greater in quantity and quality than students working independently at the computer; (b) group work promoted higher performance on factual recognition, application and problem-solving tasks than did individual work at the computer; and (c) students involved in cooperative group work:

> serve as models for each other, assist each other in analyzing and diagnosing problems, explain to each other the material being learned, teach relevant concepts and procedures to each other, keep each other on task, and share their satisfaction and sense of accomplishment with each other. (p.13)

Teaching trends, minority language students and language use

Milk (1980) found that small group settings appeared consistently to provide a highly favorable context for language use. How these groupings could promote second language acquisition, however, was not within the scope of Milk's research design. He, therefore, posed the following, insightful, questions at the end of his investigation:

> Would the amount of talk in the weaker language [i.e. L2] be increased if alternative grouping strategies were implemented in [bilingual] classrooms? Are there any treatments that involve mixing students from different language backgrounds (such as peer tutoring, or small group problem-solving),which might lead to greater use of the weaker language by all students? (pp. 133–134)

Research (e.g. Neves, 1984; Sapiens, 1982) has since been conducted which investigates the use of English and Spanish among bilingual, monolingual Spanish, and monolingual English peers within elementary and secondary small group instructional settings. These studies and others (e.g. August, 1982; Chan, 1982) found that Spanish was virtually absent among the bilinguals and present only in the logical case of speech between monolingual or near-monolingual Spanish speakers. There appear to be various possible reasons for the above language choice phenomenon. Sapiens (1982), for example, investigated 20 tutor–tutee dyads, comprised of monolingual English and bilingual tutors and partial bilingual tutees. The group mean English language proficiency scores, as assessed by BOLT[3], were virtually identical for the bilingual, monolingual, and partial bilingual subjects. Also, English was the dominant language within both the monolingual English tutor group and the partial bilingual tutee group. Moreover, the bilingual tutors' group mean scores were identical in Spanish and English, and, in the case of English, at least equivalent to the other two groups' mean scores in English. Finally, the technical nature of the topic (i.e. geography) required knowledge and manipulation of specific terminology which was not generally reflective of their interpersonal communication language use. This was especially evident in the case of those participants who spoke Spanish but who had not received formal instruction in it within this content area. Considering the above factors, the use of Spanish would not be predicted to play a significant role within such a pool of participants.

In Neves' (1984) study, verbal interaction between peers, in English and Spanish, appeared to be language proficiency-based rather than task-based. Spanish monolinguals, for example, spoke Spanish amongst themselves, while English proficient speakers spoke English amongst themselves. Those peers designated as having minimal proficiency in English and Spanish essentially were not spoken to in either language by the more proficient speakers and produced less speech than any other language group (i.e. monolingual English or Spanish, bilingual, mixed limited). Neves characterized the instructional setting she investigated as unique among science curriculum programs in that it was peer-focused and 'designed to encourage talking and working together' (p. 44), a 'fact that ... was critical' (p. 25). The setting she actually describes, however, did not meet its objectives of facilitating talk generally among peers nor was it indicative of a cooperative learning setting. Interpersonal skills among peers (and, perhaps more importantly, among the teachers and aides) appeared lacking, yet necessary to working and talking with students having different language proficiencies in English and Spanish. Interpersonal skill training was absent or ineffective, consequently there was not enough formal inducement, either by the students or, sadly, the teachers and aides, to interact with those peers who most needed language contact, and who formed as much as 44% (13 minimal and 31 mixed limited students) of Neves' study.

In the peer-tutoring research of August (1982) and Chan (1982), the bilingual students' level of English appeared sufficient for communication and perhaps was even their preferred language of communication. Thus, factors such as the language/language proficiency designation of the respective partners and even the stipulated language of the tutoring task (i.e. Spanish, as in the case of August, 1982) were overridden by the dominant role of English.

Recently, many other second language researchers (see review by Long & Porter, 1985) have investigated English language use among native- and non-native-English speakers, especially between non-native-/non-native-English speaking students. This research has introduced and manipulated important concepts which can add to the knowledge of how non-native English speakers use English (e.g. Long's (1980) two-way task concept, to be discussed below). The specific applicability of this research, however, to the various types of elementary school settings characterized earlier is severely limited. Subjects, for example, are generally adult, university undergraduates or graduates, from at least the middle class socioeconomic stratum, who are standard speakers of their first language. Also, neither the topics nor tasks generally selected reflect the natural classroom setting where children basically are involved in learning a particular content area (e.g. reading, writing, math, science, social science).

Two-way task and adult second language use

Particular methodological constructs within adult second language research, however, appear relevant in the investigation of second language use within the types of elementary and secondary settings discussed earlier. Long (1980), for example, found that significant differences only occurred in speech production among dyads where both native speakers and non-native speakers had information to contribute to the task. Long termed these types of tasks 'two way'. Where only the native speaker has information to impart—that is, a 'one-way' task—the learner does not have the opportunity to negotiate the conversation by providing verbal feedback to the native speaker. Two-way tasks in which native speech is modified and 'roughly tuned' (Krashen, 1981: 102) to that of the non-native speaker are necessary conditions, in Long's opinion, for comprehensible input. Follow-up studies by Long (1981, 1983) have corroborated that conversational modifications (i.e. input by the L2 learner) occur significantly more in two-way tasks than in one-way tasks.

One-way tasks, two-way tasks and cooperative learning: implications for L2 use

We have seen that cooperative learning has been effective in generating language use among native-language peers in regular and CAI settings. On the other hand, the two-way task (Long, 1981), arguably the principal method for generating talk between participants, has been effective in stimulating second language use, predominantly within university students attending English as a Second Language (ESL) classes. The one-way task, moreover, has generally not been effective in either of these two types of settings. The questions which remain, however, relate to regular and CAI classroom settings and the degree to which: (1) the methods used to successfully generate talk between non-native peers by current adult-oriented L2 researchers apply; and (2) cooperative learning methods encourage second language use. A description of the essential elements associated with each method will serve as the framework within which to address these questions.

As defined here, the differences between the two-way task and cooperative learning are minor. The two-way task, as defined by Long (1981), includes two of the four major essential elements required of the formal cooperative learning model described by Johnson *et al.* (1984). The element of *positive interdependence* ensures that each member of the dyad or small group needs the remaining member(s) in order to achieve the objective of the collectively assigned task. Examples of positive interdependence strategies are assigning mutual goals (i.e. goal interdependence); divisions of labor (i.e. task interdependence); dividing materials, resources, or information among group members (resource interdependence); assigning students different roles (role interdependence); and giving joint rewards (reward interdependence). The two-way task of Long (1981, 1983) and related subsequent second language research (e.g. Doughty & Pica, 1984: Gass & Varonis, 1985) is characterized by each participant having information that the other needs in order to resolve a particular task, and is a clear example of resource interdependence.

The second element is *face-to-face interaction* among students. The importance of integrating this element with positive interdependence and educational outcomes has been stated by Johnson *et al.* (1984) in the following manner:

> There is no magic in positive interdependence in and of itself. It is the interaction patterns and verbal interchange among students promoted by positive interdependence that affect educational outcomes. (p. 8)

Face-to-face interactions are also an indispensable feature used to promote second language use among non-native speakers in recent second language discourse research (e.g. Doughty & Pica, 1984; Gass & Varonis, 1985; Long, 1981, 1983; Pica & Doughty, 1985; Porter, 1983). Moreover, the above quote appears to closely follow Long's (1981, 1983) perception of the two-way task as the optimum type of setting for language generation between two (or more) participants.

The third element is *individual accountability*, that is, participants knowing that each is responsible for mastering a particular aspect of the assigned material. Determining each student's level of mastery, therefore, is essential to the cooperative enterprise, especially with respect to the help each student can be expected to provide one's peers. This element has not been addressed within the notion of the two-way task as applied in second language research settings. Specifically, the second language research did not apprise learners of their respective levels of mastery (e.g. particular language strengths, particular task strengths, etc.) nor of the explicit objective of the two-way task assignment (e.g. sustained communication involving both speakers as a means to improving L2 proficiency).

Finally, students should receive training in how to cooperate as well as feedback with respect to how well they are cooperating. Thus, the *interpersonal* and *small-group skills* associated with effective cooperative learning must be identified, transmitted, reinforced, and evaluated. Examples of these social skills include leadership, ability to communicate, trust of others, and conflict management. This training has not been formally present in the second language research settings, including those involving the two-way task, mentioned here.

The one-way task, on the other hand, appears to incorporate but one of the four essential elements of the cooperative learning model described, the element of face-to-face interaction. However, the incorporation of this element is incomplete, for while it is the case that the students are face-to-face, it is not necessarily the case that there is interaction. Thus, as demonstrated in the research of Neves (1984), five groupings based on differential English and Spanish language proficiencies (i.e. monolingual English, monolingual Spanish, bilinguals, limited mixed language, and minimal language) did not interact with each other in either language. This resulted in a virtual-to-near verbal ostracism by the three more proficient language groups of the two lowest language proficiency groups (i.e. minimal language and mixed limited), who formed 13% and 34% respectively, of the study's ninety-nine (99) participants. Furthermore, as evinced in the research by August (1982), even face-to-face groupings with one-way training (i.e. of only one of the two or more participants) has not resulted in interaction in the desired language (in this case, Spanish between groups of two bilinguals of differential Spanish language proficiency). In summary, when the element of positive interdependence is absent, the mere grouping of peers with differential language proficiencies does not appear to result in enhanced L2, or, to use Milk's (1980) term, weaker language, use. This appears to occur even when training is given to one of the peers forming part of a dyad.

Conversely, August's (1982) study demonstrated that when both peers were trained relative to how and when to interact with one another (i.e. a two-way role-interdependent type situation complemented by cooperative training), interaction in the L2 (English) by the limited English speakers increased significantly.

Second language use within a CAI, two-way task learning setting

Research has been cited which clearly indicates that language interaction between peers plays a significant role within the computerized learning context. Spoken language between peers is prevalent, moreover, in all types of computer activities, whether structured for individualized or small group instruction (Becker, 1984/85). As illustrated earlier, performance is also enhanced when students work together at the computer (Johnson *et al.*, 1985). Until very recently, however, research had not been conducted with regard to second language use between peers involved in a two-way task within a CAI learning setting. To address this question, DeVillar (1987) investigated the language use (i.e. English, Spanish, intra-sentential code-switching) within and between dyads, who were engaged in a two-way task, CAI learning setting within a sixth grade classroom. This research strongly suggests a more viable alternative to the traditional methods of instruction already discussed. A summary of his research follows.

Methodology

Four pairs of speakers, all male, were matched according to a different English language proficiency level, i.e. monolingual English (ME), full English proficiency (FEP), limited English proficiency (LEP), and non-English proficient (NEP).[4] The two native English speakers were white, non-Hispanic. After each matched language proficiency dyad was observed, mixed language proficiency dyads were formed by arbitrarily selecting one speaker from each matched language proficiency dyad and pairing them with one another.[5] A total of ten dyad combinations (i.e. 4 matched pairs; 6 mixed pairs), then, were formed, observed, and videotaped. Each dyad was observed on 4 occasions of 20 minutes each. In this way, four of the eight speakers participated in both matched and mixed dyads, and, for purposes of analysis, identified as target speakers. This design ensured that target speakers from each level of English proficiency participated in a dyad combination with target speakers from all other English proficiency levels, as well as with a speaker having their own level of English proficiency. The research intent was to determine to what extent a target speaker's language use varied in accordance with the English language proficiency of his partner.

Positive interdependence was established through the use of a task interdependence strategy. Thus, one student was responsible for all computer keyboard entries for half of each observation period (10 minutes), while his partner was responsible, during that same period, for observing that all entries on the computer screen were grammatically correct and accurately reflected the mutually agreed upon content, as well as for reading all text instructions printed on the screen. The software package used was an English language version of *Bank Street Writer* (Scholastic, Inc., New York, 1984, Apple version).[6] At the end of the first half of each observation session (i.e. 10 minutes), the partners would switch task responsibilities for the remainder of the observation session. Thus, both tasks were shared equally by the participants during each observation session.

Prior to beginning the first observation for each dyad, the investigator provided a 10–15 minute introduction to the dyad members, informing them of (1) the cooperative nature of the learning activity, (2) each member's task assignment, (3) the need to switch tasks at 10 minute intervals, (4) the fact that talk was encouraged between participants, and (5) the particular lesson activity. During subsequent sessions with the same dyads, only steps (2), (3) and (5) were transmitted to them by the researcher.

Speech from the forty observation sessions was transcribed,[7] words counted, and utterances segmented into (a) T-units (Hunt, 1964) modified to incorporate command sentences and uninverted questions (Bloomfield, 1933), and (b) fragments.[8] Neither oral reading nor speech directed at the researcher (a sporadic phenomenon) was included in the final transcriptions as the former was considered language-like behavior (Milk, 1980) and the latter was considered extraneous to the purpose of the study.

Data analysis

A general descriptive statistical analysis of the criterion variable 'word count' was conducted, followed by analysis of variance (ANOVA) with *post hoc* comparisons (i.e. Student–Newman–Keuls technique). Only observation sessions one and four were analyzed due to the unexpectedly large corpus of talk generated (i.e. approximately 15,000 T-units and fragments).

A. Results: dyad level

1. *General word-count.* The ten dyad combinations produced 18,130 words during observation sessions one and four, reflecting 6 hours and 40 minutes of working together. Consequently, dyads averaged 45 words of speech per minute. This type of learning setting, then, was highly conducive to language production.

2. *The role of English.* Generally, English was the predominant language used by the dyads in their talk to one another, accounting for 15,669 words, or 86% of all words produced. Combining all three language categories (English, Spanish, intra-sentential code-switching), overall language production was positively associated with the English language proficiency (ELP) of each of the interlocutors within the dyad: the higher the ELP of each interlocutor, the more words produced within the dyad.

3. *Fluency in English and dyad grouping: relative effects on word-counts.* At comparable ELP matched dyad levels (i.e. native English speaking dyad and fully English proficient dyad), the FEP dyad produced more words, including English words, than did the native English speaking dyad. Within mixed dyads, however, more words were always produced with a native English speaking partner than with an FEP partner. Generally, dyads, regardless of ELP, produced more language when comprised of two speakers with the same ELP (i.e. matched dyad), than when comprised of one of those same speakers and a partner from any other ELP designation (i.e. mixed dyad).

4. *Utterance type preferences.* Dyads predominantly spoke to each other in utterances categorized as simple and complex sentences. Almost half (49%) of all words in English and the majority of words (61%) in Spanish, for example, were within the simple sentence category. Dyads produced 9% of all words in the form of complex sentences, predominantly in English (92%). Less than 2% (281) of all words were in the form of isolated subordinate clauses (clausal fragments), 95% of which were in English. Words in the form of one-word responses or other non-clausal fragments accounted for 39% (7,025) of all words produced, 89% of which were in

English. Thus utterances were generally syntactically complete, grammatically appropriate units spoken in English.

5. *Spanish*. Spanish words accounted for 12% of all words and were generally limited (94%) to dyads comprised of at least one NEP speaker. In general, word-count in Spanish was inversely associated with the ELP of each of the interlocutors: the lower the ELP, the higher the language production in Spanish.

6. *Code-switching*. Mixed language accounted for less than 2% of all language produced and, as Spanish, was inversely associated with the ELP of each of the interlocutors within the dyad.

B. Results: target speaker level

1. *The role of English and English language proficiency*. English was the predominant language used by all target speakers, regardless of ELP designation. Generally, the higher the ELP of the speaker, the higher the percentage of English used. Thus, the ME speaker produced 100% of his talk in English; the FEP speaker, 89%; the LEP speaker, 89%; and the NEP speaker, 57%. A higher percentage of English use, however, did not necessarily equate to speaking more English. In fact, the FEP speaker produced 10% more words in English than the ME speaker; likewise, but only at the matched dyad level, the LEP speaker also produced more English than did the ME speaker. Conversely, the NEP speaker produced 4 times less English than his ME target speaking counterpart, 4.5 less than his FEP counterpart, and 3.7 times less than his LEP counterpart.

2. *The effect of grouping by English language proficiency*

(a) *Overall language level*. All target speakers produced more overall language when paired with their matched language proficiency counterparts. Thus, at the overall language level, all were sensitive to the differential ELP designations of their interlocutors and responded in the same way, i.e. by lowering the quantity of their language production.

(b) *English language level*. In English the effect of the native English speaking interlocutor on the English language production of the non-native English (NNE) target speakers was inversely associated with the ELP designation of his partner. That is, the lower the ELP of the NNE target speaker, the less the percentage differential between his word-count at the matched dyad level and the word-count he produced within his mixed dyad involving the native English speaking interlocutor. Thus, the difference between the amount of words in English that the FEP speaker produced within his matched dyad and that which he produced with his native English speaking counterpart was 41% less. For the LEP speaker, it was 37% less. And, in the case of the NEP speaker, there was an 8% increase in

English word production. This last phenomenon did not occur within any other mixed dyad.

(c)   *Language use in mixed dyads.* There were two important behaviors associated with the native English speaker within mixed dyads. First, the non-native English target speakers produced more language when paired with the native English speaker than with any combination involving another non-native English speaker of a different ELP designation. Moreover, non-native English target speakers, when paired with the native English speaking interlocutor, only spoke in English.

Within mixed dyads in general, the higher ELP speaker always produced a higher percentage of talk in English than the lower ELP speaker. This pattern was especially visible at the NEP mixed dyad level where between 72% and 76% of all English was produced by his three higher ELP partners.

3. *Utterance complexity and grouping strategies.* The two patterns described above—NNE speakers within mixed dyads speaking more English with the native English speaker and the NEP speaker producing even more English with the ME than within his matched proficiency dyad—were also evident at the T-unit and fragment level. That is, NNE speakers produced more simple sentences with the ME speaker than with any mixed dyad combination, and the NEP speaker produced a higher percentage of simple sentences in English with the ME speaker than within his matched language proficiency dyad.

4. *Task assignment and language use*

(a)   *Overall effect.* Target speakers as a group produced more words at the screen task (54%) than at the keyboard task (46%). At the screen, the ME and FEP speakers produced 58% and 57%, respectively, while the NEP produced 45% and the LEP, 50%.

(b)   *Effect by English language proficiency level.* From keyboard to screen, the NEP speaker experienced a 44% decrease in the use of English and a 33% increase in both the use of Spanish and mixed language, coupled by an overall 10% reduction in the number of words. The ME and FEP, in contrast, both substantially increased their word production from keyboard to screen.

(c)   *Input differentials by English language proficiency.* The fragment input to the NEP target speaker increased by 86% in the case of the ME and by 48% in the case of the FEP. The FEP speaker's input to the NEP, moreover, was mainly produced in Spanish and mixed language both at the screen (60%) and at the keyboard (55%). Input from keyboard to screen by the LEP speaker to the NEP speaker was also characterized by a greater percentage of fragments with a decrease in the percentage of simple sentences.

C. Results: speech complexity and adjustment among target speakers

A target speaker's speech complexity was generally uniform across his various interlocutors, regardless of their ELP designation. That is, there was generally no statistically significant variation (i.e. adjustment) in the mean lengths of T-units or fragments which a target speaker produced when speaking to his four interlocutors. However, when significant adjustment did occur, it was generally downward and dependent upon interacting contextual elements rather than solely on the ELP of the interlocutor. In this setting, the interacting elements were task type (screen or keyboard), language choice (English, Spanish, or mixed language), and speech production type (simple or complex sentence or fragment), together with the ELP designation of the interlocutor.

The strongest indication of a consistent speech simplification pattern (i.e. downward adjustment) was demonstrated by the native English speaker (ME). At the fragment level, whenever he encountered a non-native English speaker, regardless of the latter's level of ELP, he would significantly simplify his speech from the level which he used with his matched native English speaking partner. Also, at the simple sentence level, the native English speaker simplified his speech whenever he spoke *at the screen* with his NEP interlocutor.

Although speech adjustment was generally downward, it was upward on four occasions. On three of the four occasions, the adjustments were made by the NEP speaker. On two of the three occasions, he made adjustments at the simple sentence utterance level in English, while he was at the screen task with his ME and LEP counterparts. Thus, upward adjustment typically occurred at the lowest ELP level and on an exceptional basis. Furthermore, it was not predicated solely on the criterion of the interlocutor's degree of ELP, but upon ELP in interaction with the variables of task (i.e. screen) and speech production type (simple sentence).

Summary

The implications relative to second language opportunities within the classroom, then, may be divided into two related general categories: (a) dyad grouping strategies and (b) task assignment within dyads.

Grouping strategies by English language proficiency level

1. *Overall words in English.* English was virtually the language of communication whenever ME, FEP, and LEP speakers were involved with one

another in matched or mixed dyads. Word-count among speakers from these three language proficiency designations was comparable, although the FEP almost uniformly produced more words at all levels than did the native English speaker. Moreover, the FEP and LEP speakers generally used their Spanish or mixed language only when communicating with their NEP interlocutor rather than with each other. The NEP speaker, on the other hand, was very sensitive to interlocutor effect in that he not only used English with the native English speaker but also produced the largest number of words when paired with the native English speaker.

Thus, within dyad situations at the 6th grade level, substantial English language practice (both input and output) is possible through the use of non-native English speakers at the LEP and FEP levels in matched (LEP–LEP, FEP–FEP) and mixed (ME–FEP, ME–LEP, FEP–LEP) dyads. At the NEP speaker level, however, perhaps the dyad partner who will contribute maximally to his practice in English language input and output is only the native English speaker, as the NEP speaker's speech at this level is fully in English and quantitatively greater than with any other interlocutor.

2. *Syntactic production in English.* Speakers at the limited English proficient and fully English proficient levels, within their matched dyads, produced both a higher percentage of their speech in English and more simple sentences in English than did the native English speaker. The non-English proficient speaker, on the other hand, neither produced as many simple sentences in English nor did the total which he produced compare on a percentage basis with that which the ME had produced. Thus, at the LEP and FEP speaker levels, English language output was strongly in the form of simple sentences, while at the NEP speaker level, it was characterized more by fragments.

In mixed dyad groupings, however, the native English speaker played an important role as interlocutor. The LEP and FEP speakers, for example, produced more simple sentences in English with their native English speaking partner than they did when speaking with any non-native English speaking partner within a mixed dyad. Similarly, the NEP speaker produced more simple sentences with the native English speaking partner than with any non-native English speaking interlocutor. An important difference, however, was that the NEP speaker produced more simple sentences with his native English speaking partner than he had produced when speaking to his matched proficiency interlocutor.

Within a cooperative-type instructional setting, dyads comprised of ME, FEP, and LEP speakers in matched and mixed combinations will produce substantial portions of their speech, at times even most of their speech, in the form of simple sentences. Insofar as production of simple sentences by the NEP speaker, he may profit most from collaboration with a native English speaker. Not only did the NEP speaker generate more words as simple sentences in English within this grouping, but he also produced a higher percentage of his total English speech as simple sentences.

3. *Input and output in English.* As has been indicated, the quantities of English produced by the LEP and FEP speakers are comparable, if not greater than, those produced by the native English speaker, irrespective of dyad grouping. The NEP speaker, however, produced only 30% of his total speech in English within his matched dyad. Moreover, at the mixed dyad level, the English language speech produced by the NEP speaker to any one of his interlocutors represented approximately 25% of the total English speech produced by the dyad. While higher English language proficiency was related to percentage of English spoken, this pattern was strongest at the NEP level.

Thus, it appears that the NEP participant will uniformly receive more than he produces. Also, the percentage of English produced by the NEP speaker did not vary appreciably as his partners changed within the mixed dyad groupings. Thus, at the mixed dyad level, enhanced percentage of talk in English by the NEP speaker does not appear to depend on the English language proficiency of the interlocutor. Consequently, dyad grouping strategies perhaps should be designed relative to other criteria, such as those factors presented above and discussed below.

Task assignment and English language production

1. *General production of English.* While speakers generally produced more words in English at the screen task than at the keyboard task, the opposite was true for the NEP speaker. Thus, for the NEP speaker, the screen task generally provided more opportunity for English input while the keyboard task provided more opportunity for English output. Hence, teachers may wish to alternate the NEP speaker's placement at the screen or keyboard relative to the type of English language practice from which they wish this speaker to benefit.

2. *Task assignment and English language complexity.* The native English speaker tended to adjust his speech in relation to the type of utterance he was producing or the particular task for which he had responsibility in conjunction with, rather than solely on the basis of, the English language proficiency of his interlocutor. Specifically, he adjusted his speech to all

non-native English speakers, irrespective of his task responsibility, but only at the fragment level and not at the simple or complex sentence levels. At the screen, the native English speaker extended his speech adjustment to include simple sentences when talking to the NEP interlocutor.

Thus, where less complex talk at the native English speaking level is desired, dyad grouping strategies involving the native English speaker should consider the English language proficiency of the interlocutor, together with task assignment, and the potential type of utterances which may be simplified.

The non-native English speaker adjusted upward the complexity of his simple sentences in English, while at the screen task, to his ME and LEP interlocutors. Hence, English language opportunities may be enhanced for speakers at this proficiency level by consideration of specific task placement in combination with particular interlocutors.

Grouping strategies for Spanish language use

Where native Spanish speakers are encouraged to maintain or develop their Spanish language while learning English, mixed dyads comprised of non-native speakers, especially where a non-English proficiency speaker participates, would likely produce substantial quantities of Spanish. Furthermore, in a Spanish language oriented instructional setting, the use of Spanish could perhaps be enhanced considerably by using appropriate Spanish language software. Similarly, where native English speakers are encouraged to learn Spanish within an instructional setting (e.g. Spanish immersion program, two-way bilingual program), dyad groupings involving native Spanish speakers who are either fully English proficient or limited English proficient would perhaps provide substantial Spanish language opportunities where appropriate Spanish language software were utilized.

Grouping strategies and educational objectives

Perhaps the most general implication having relevance to the classroom comprised of students having different English language proficiency levels concerns grouping dyads in relation to the particular learning objectives of the teacher. For example, in the event that the primary objective for a particular time period were second language learning opportunities within the subject matter classroom, then grouping the lower English proficiency speakers with the native English speakers would appear appropriate. If, on the other hand, the primary objective for a particular time period were subject matter learning or reinforcement, then grouping students in mixed non-native English proficiency dyads would possibly be more effective. Both of the above types of learning objectives, of course, could be set during the same time period. Thus, dyad groupings (to include matched language proficiency pairs at all levels of proficiency) could alternate in accordance with the particular learning objectives of the teachers over the course of the school year.

Given the evidence provided by the DeVillar study, it is proposed that dyad groupings of the type presented here could become an effective addition to teachers' existing classroom instructional practices, thereby enhancing the opportunities for language minority students to acquire school-related English proficiency within a cooperative, peer-oriented instructional setting, and, by extension, the probability of succeeding academically.

Notes to Chapter 8

1. English language proficiency, albeit of major importance, is of course only one factor exerting influence on an individual's educational attainment. Other factors to consider, individually and in combination, relate to the socioeconomic, cultural, political, physical, psychological, and educational circumstances within which the individual acts and is acted upon (i.e. interacts), both as an individual and as a social being.
2. The intent of the Bilingual Education Act (1968) was to teach non- and limited-English speaking children English so that it would replace their first language in all school activities, and, by extension, beyond school activities (see Rodolfo Jacobson, 1982).
3. Bahia Oral Language Test (BOLT) assesses oral language fluency in Spanish and English through separate BOLT versions. Test is administered individually, employs pictures to elicit language, and is designed to measure knowledge of the grammatical structures of English or Spanish.
4. Language Assessment Scale (LAS) scores were made available to the researcher to determine students' individual English and Spanish language proficiency levels. These scores were complemented by students' outcomes on a Home Language Survey (HLS), the English version of the Comprehensive Test of Basic Skills (CTBS), and a teacher checklist questionnaire (SOLOM), in order to ensure that LAS scores were currently (i.e. March, 1986) indicative of the students' actual English language proficiency levels.
5. The remaining four speakers who initially formed part of the four matched dyads and who, by process of arbitrary selection, were not selected to participate in mixed dyads, no longer were involved in the study. Their initial presence in the

study enabled the researcher to gather baseline language data on each speaker at his particular level of language proficiency. The baseline data then served as a comparison point from which to judge variation which might have occurred in any one speaker as he spoke to partners having greater or lesser English language proficiency.

This strategy was selected for two reasons. First, by reducing the number of subjects from a potential 20 (i.e. 10 dyad combinations multiplied by two peers per dyad) to eight, the amount of data collection per individual was increased, while the number of dyad groupings remained the same. Second, by having had the same individuals participate in different dyad combinations, comparison of how an individual's speech behavior varied along designated factors from one particular English language proficiency category (e.g. LEP) to any other (e.g. monolingual English, FEP, NEP) was facilitated. This latter analysis was considered fundamental to the central research focus and would not have been possible under the alternative design stipulation that each dyad combination be comprised of a different subject.

6. The BSW is essentially a menu-driven word processing program designed to help K–6 students in their language arts skills development. It specifically engages students in activities requiring typing and editing of stories, worksheets, and articles. Tasks include insertion/deletion of letters, words, and paragraphs; movement of paragraphs; typing of class, group, or language experience stories. It was selected because the participants had used the package on various occasions over the course of the prior semester, thereby eliminating the need for their learning an unfamiliar language arts software package solely for this study.

7. All talk was freely transcribed, using conventional English and Spanish spelling for words spoken. Segmentation of talk for purposes of analysis was based on T-unit and fragment definitions cited below (see endnote #8). No other grammatical (e.g. punctuation), linguistic (e.g. phonetic/phonemic notations), paralinguistic (e.g. speech tempo, rhythm or quality), or discourse analysis (e.g. speech acts) conventions or methods were systematically applied to the data for purposes of analysis.

8. Originally developed by Kellog W. Hunt (1964) to measure the syntactic development (i.e. 'maturity') in the writing of 4th, 8th and 12th graders, the Minimal Terminable Unit, or T-unit, was defined as 'one main clause plus whatever subordinate clauses and nonclausal expressions are attached to or embedded within it' (Hunt, 1970: 14). A single T-unit, therefore, is equivalent to a simple sentence (e.g. 'Now you read.') or complex sentence (e.g. 'I was thinking it was something else.'), while a compound sentence would be regarded as two T-units (e.g. 'Now press return and keep on pressing it.'). As early as 1967, the T-unit had been used to measure oral syntactic development of native English speakers (e.g. O'Donnell, Griffin & Norris, 1967), and, by 1969, that of Spanish-speaking students in the U.S. (e.g. Amsden, 1969, Thornhill, 1969). It remains a widely used measure of oral syntactic development among current second language acquisition researchers (e.g. Beebe, 1983; Larsen-Freeman, 1983; Long, 1981, 1985).

One-word responses (e.g. 'yes'/'no'), subordinate clauses in isolation from a main clause (e.g. 'Because they get nervous.') (after Ramirez, 1974), and other structurally incomplete talk (see Bowman, 1966), were categorized as fragments.

Bibliography

AMSDEN, C.E. 1969, A study of the syntax of oral English by thirty selected Mexican-American children, three to five years old in a preschool setting. Unpublished Doctoral Dissertation, Claremont Graduate School and University Center.

AUGUST, D.L. 1982, The effects of peer tutoring on the second language acquisition of Hispanic elementary school children. Unpublished Doctoral Dissertation, Stanford University.

BECKER, H.J. 1984/1985, School uses of microcomputers: Report #6 from a national survey. *Journal of Computers in Mathematics and Science Teaching* 4(2), 42–9.

BEEBE, L.M. 1983, Risk-taking and the language learner. In H.W. SELIGER and M.H. LONG (eds), *Classroom Oriented Research in Language Acquisition* pp. 39–65. Rowley, Massachusetts: Newbury House.

BLOOMFIELD, L. 1933, *Language*. New York: Holt.

BOWMAN, E. 1966, *The Minor and Fragmentary Sentences of a Corpus of Spoken English*. Bloomington, Indiana: Indiana University.

CHAN, V.O. 1982, The discourse patterns of bilingual and monolingual mathematic tutors: Effects on mathematics achievement of bilingual Chicano students. Unpublished Doctoral Dissertation, Stanford University.

COHEN, E.G. 1986, *Designing Groupwork: Strategies for the Heterogeneous Classroom*. New York: Teachers College Press.

CUMMINS, J. 1981, The role of primary language development in promoting educational success for language minority students. In Office of Bilingual Bicultural Education (ed.), *Schooling and Language Minority Students: A Theoretical Framework* (pp. 3–49). Los Angeles, CA.: Evaluation, Dissemination and Assessment Center (California State University).

DE AVILA, E.A., DUNCAN, S.E., ULIBARRI, D.M. and FLEMING, J.S. 1983, Predicting the academic success of minority language students from developmental, cognitive style, linguistic and teacher perception measures. In E.E. GARCIA (ed.), *The Mexican American Child, Language, Cognition and Social Development*. (pp. 59–105). Tempe, Arizona: Center for Bilingual Education.

Department of Education and Science 1975, *A Language for Life* (The Bullock Report). London: HMSO.

DEVILLAR, R.A. 1987, Variation in the language use of peer dyads within a bilingual, cooperative, computer-assisted instructional setting. Unpublished Doctoral Dissertation, Stanford University.

DICKSON, W.P. and VEREEN, M.A. 1983, Two students at one microcomputer. *Theory Into Practice* 22(4), 296–300.

DOUGHTY, C. and PICA, T. 1984, Small group work in the ESL classroom: does it facilitate language acquisition? Paper presented at TESOL 1984. Houston, Texas.

ENRIGHT, D.S. and MCCLOSKEY, M.L. 1985, Yes, talking!: organizing the classroom to promote second language acquisition. *TESOL Quarterly* 19(3), 431–53.

FERGUSON, C. and HEATH, S.B. 1981 On TESOL and language in American life. In J.C. FISHER, M.A. CLARKE and J. SCHACTER (eds), *On TESOL '80, Building Bridges: Research and Practice in Teaching English as a Second Language* (pp. 28–37). Washington DC: TESOL, 1981.

FLANDERS, N. 1970, *Analyzing Teaching Behaviour*. London: Addison-Wesley.
GASS, S.M. and VARONIS, E.M. 1985, Task variation and nonnative/nonnative negotiation of meaning. In S.M. GASS and C.G. MADDEN (eds), *Input in Second Language Acquisition* (pp. 149–61). Rowley, Massachusetts: Newbury House Publishers.
GOODLAD, J.I. 1986, Foreword. In E.G. COHEN, *Designing Groupwork Strategies for the Heterogeneous Classroom*. New York: Teachers College Press.
HAWKINS, J. 1984, The interpretation of LOGO in practice. Technical Report, Center for Children and Technology, Bank Street College of Education.
HERNANDEZ-CHAVEZ, E. 1984, The inadequacy of English immersion education as an educational approach for language in the United States. In Office of Bilingual Bicultural Education (ed.), *Studies on Immersion Education, A Collection for United States Educators*. (pp. 144–183). Sacramento, CA: California State Department of Education.
HUNT, K.W. 1964, Differences in grammatical structures written at three grade levels, the structures to be analyzed by transformational methods. Technical Report, Cooperative Research Project No. 1998. Tallahassee: Florida State University.
—— 1970, *Syntactic Maturity in School Children and Adults*. Monographs of the Society for Research in Child Development, 35.
JACOBSON, R. 1982, The role of the vernacular in transitional bilingual education. In B. HARTFORD, A. VALDMAN and C.R. FOSTER (eds), *Issues in International Bilingual Education, The Role of the Vernacular*. New York: Plenum Press.
JOHNSON, D.W. and JOHNSON, R.T. 1983, The socialization and achievement crises: Are cooperative learning experiences the solution? In L. BICKMAN (ed.), *Applied Social Psychology Annual 4*. Beverly Hills, CA.: Sage.
JOHNSON, D.W., MARUYAMA, G., JOHNSON, R., NELSON, D. and SKON, L. 1981, Effects of cooperative, competitive, and individualistic goal structures on achievement: a meta-analysis. *Psychological Bulletin* 89, 47–62.
JOHNSON, D.W., JOHNSON, R.T., HOLUBEC JOHNSON, E. and ROY, P. 1984, *Circles of Learning, Cooperation in the Classroom*. Alexandria, Virginia: Association for Supervision and Curriculum Development.
JOHNSON, D.W., JOHNSON, R.T. and STANNE, M. 1985, Effects of cooperative, competitive, and individualistic goal structures on computer-assisted instruction. *Journal of Educational Psychology* 77(6), 668–77.
KLEIN, W. 1986, *Second Language Acquisition*. Cambridge, England: Cambridge University Press.
KRASHEN, S.D. 1981, *Second Language Acquisition and Second Language Learning*. Oxford, England: Pergamon Press.
—— 1982, *Principles and Practice in Second Language Acquisition*. Oxford, England: Pergamon Press.
LARSEN-FREEMAN, D. 1983, Assessing global second language proficiency. In H.W. SELIGER and M.H. LONG (eds), *Classroom Oriented Research in Second Language Acquisition* (pp. 287–304). Rowley, Massachusetts: Newbury House Publishers.
LEVIN, H.L. 1985, The educationally disadvantaged: A national crisis. Program Report No. 85-B1, Institute for Research on Educational Finance and Governance, School of Education, Stanford University. Philadelphia, Pennsylvania: Center for the State Youth Initiatives of Public/Private Ventures.

LITTLEWOOD, W. 1981, *Communicative Language Teaching, An Introduction.* Cambridge, England: Cambridge University Press, 7th printing (1986).

LONG, M.H. 1980, Input, interaction and second language acquisition. Unpublished Doctoral Dissertation, University of California at Los Angeles.

—— 1981, Input, interaction, and second language acquisition. In H. WINITZ (ed.), *Native Language and Foreign Language Acquisition.* Annals of the New York Academy of Sciences 379, 250–78.

—— 1983, Native speakers/non-native speaker conversation in the second language classroom. In M. CLARKE and J. HANDSCOMBE (eds), *On TESOL '82: Pacific Perspectives on Language Learning and Teaching.* Washington, DC: TESOL.

—— 1985, Input and second language acquisition theory. In S.M. GASS and C.G. MADDEN (eds), *Input in Second Language Acquisition.* Rowley, MA: Newbury House.

LONG, M.H. and PORTER, P. 1985, Group work, interlanguage talk, and second language acquisition. *TESOL Quarterly* 19(2), 207–28.

LONG, M. and SATO, C. 1983, Classroom foreigner talk discourse: forms and functions of teachers' questions. In H.W. SELIGER and M.H. LONG (eds), *Classroom Oriented Research in Language Acquisition.* (pp. 268–285). Rowley, Massachusetts: Newbury House.

MEHAN, H. 1979, *Learning Lessons: Social Organization in the Classroom.* Cambridge, Massachusetts: Harvard University Press.

MILK, R. 1980, Variations in language use patterns across different group settings in two bilingual second grade classrooms. Unpublished Doctoral Dissertation, Stanford University.

NEVES, H.A. 1984, Talking in the classroom and second language acquisition. Unpublished Doctoral Dissertation, Stanford University.

O'DONNELL, R.C., GRIFFIN, W.J. and NORRIS, R.C. 1967, *Syntax of Kindergarten and Elementary Schoolchildren: A Transformation Analysis.* Champaign, Illinois.

OXFORD-CARPENTER, R., POL, L., LOPEZ, D., STUPP, P., GENDELL, M. and PENG, S. 1984, *Demographic Projections of Non-English-Background and Limited-English-Proficient Persons in the United States to the Year 2000 by State, Age, and Language Group.* Rosslyn, Virginia: Inter-American Research Associates, Inc.

PICA, T. and DOUGHTY, C. 1985, Input and interaction in the communicative language classroom: a comparison of teacher-fronted and group activities. In S.M. GASS and C.G. MADDEN (eds), *Input in Second Language Acquisition.* Rowley, MA: Newbury House.

PORTER, P. 1983, Variations in the conversations of adult learners of English as a function of the proficiency level of the participants. Unpublished Doctoral Dissertation, Stanford University.

RAMIREZ, A.G. 1974, The spoken English of Spanish-speaking pupils in a bilingual and monolingual school setting: An analysis of syntactic development. Unpublished Doctoral Dissertation, Stanford University.

—— 1985, *Bilingualism Through Schooling: Cross-Cultural Education for Minority and Majority Students.* Albany, New York: State University of New York Press.

RICHARDS, J.C. and RODGERS, T.S. 1986, *Approaches and Methods in Language Teaching, A Description and Analysis.* Cambridge, England: Cambridge University Press.

RUBIN, J. 1975, What the 'good language learner' can teach us. *TESOL Quarterly* 9(1), 41–51.

SAPIENS, A. 1982, Instructional language strategies in bilingual Chicano peer tutoring and their effect on cognitive and affective learning outcomes. Unpublished Doctoral Dissertation, Stanford University.

SEELEY, D.S. 1985, *Education Through Partnership*. Washington, DC: American Enterprise Institute for Public Policy Research.

SLAVIN, R.E. 1983, Non-cognitive outcomes of cooperative learning. In J.M. LEVINE and M.C. WANG (eds), *Teacher and Student Perceptions: Implications for Learning*. (pp. 341–65). Hillsdale, New Jersey: Lawrence Erlbaum Associates, Publishers.

STEIN, C.B. 1986, *Sink or Swim, The Politics of Bilingual Education*. New York: Praeger Publishers.

THORNHILL, D.E. 1969, A quantitative analysis of the development of syntactical fluency of four young adult Spanish speakers learning English. Unpublished doctoral dissertation, Florida State University.

WALKER, C.L. and RAKOW, S.J. 1985, The status of Hispanic American students in science: Attitudes. *Hispanic Journal of Behavioral Sciences* 7(3), 225–45.

WILLIG, A.C. 1985, A meta-analysis of selected studies on the effectiveness of bilingual education. *Review of Educational Research* 55(3), 269–317.

Section IV
Special Cases

9 Teacher Quechua use in bilingual and non-bilingual classrooms of Puno, Peru

NANCY H. HORNBERGER

In 1980, the Experimental Bilingual Education Project of Puno (PEEB) began work in schools of rural Quechua-speaking communities of Puno, Peru. The project introduced the use of Quechua as a medium of instruction into schools where Spanish had traditionally been the only official language of instruction. The majority of the rural school population in Puno arrives at school speaking only Quechua. Although some use of Quechua had always occurred in these schools, the PEEB project introduced the first systematic use of Quechua in Puno schools (see Hornberger, 1988 for more detail).

Jacobson (1987) has argued that the allocation of the two languages in a bilingual program is a key feature of that program's methodology. That is, the use of a concurrent, separating or merging distributional pattern between the languages in a bilingual program is an indicator of the overall approach of the program towards the languages and the children's learning. Thus, in this case, the way Quechua is used in the PEEB bilingual classrooms not only differentiates them from the non-bilingual classrooms but also is an indicator of the type of bilingual education the PEEB is implementing.

This chapter compares and contrasts teacher Quechua use in a PEEB and a non-PEEB school in an attempt to understand what difference the PEEB project made in language use in the classroom and ultimately in children's learning. My approach in considering the impact of the PEEB project in the classroom and the school is an ethnographic description in which criteria are drawn from the context itself, rather than being externally imposed (cf. Spindler, 1982: 6–7). The data for this chapter come from a two-year ethnographic study carried out primarily, although not exclusively, in two rural Quechua-speaking communities of Puno, Kinsachata and Visallani. The PEEB project was in operation in the former community, but not in the latter.

In the sections which follow, I describe teacher Quechua use in the classroom during lesson time in terms of (1) amount of Quechua use, (2) types of teacher talk realized in Quechua, and (3) types of code-switching between Quechua and Spanish. I treat first the traditional, non-bilingual classroom setting, and then the bilingual PEEB classroom setting. Underlying the whole discussion of teacher Quechua use is the implication that the quality and extent of teachers' use of the L1 has significant effects on children's L1 language development.

Teacher Quechua use in non-bilingual classrooms

At Kinsachata, Visallani and a third community, Pumiti, I became well acquainted with 12 teachers and three initial education (*Wawa Wasi*) promoters. Over a period of six months each in Kinsachata and Visallani and one month in Pumiti, I observed their language use on a daily basis in their work and to some extent in their recreation and free time. Though the proportion of Quechua-speaking teachers was high (80%) in these communities, it became clear that the teachers' ability to speak Quechua was not a reliable indicator of whether Quechua was used in class. Of the 13 non-PEEB teachers observed, seven were *never* observed to use Quechua in class, and four used it only rarely, that is, only once or twice during all my observations. Interestingly enough, the remaining two non-PEEB teachers who used Quechua somewhat more than their colleagues, spoke Quechua as a second and not as a first language.

Let us consider the amount and type of Quechua use in class by the above-mentioned six non-PEEB teachers. As to the amount of Quechua use, four of these teachers used it only rarely. For example, out of 860 minutes of class lesson time observed over a period of six months in Profesor Gregorio's class, there were only four instances of Quechua utterances by Profesor Gregorio.[1] Furthermore, the two teachers who used somewhat more Quechua still did not use it for any significant proportion of the total time. Out of 1,175 minutes of observed lesson time in Sra Sara's first and second grade class over a period of six months, for example, I recorded 31 instances of Quechua utterances. Out of the 675 minutes of lesson time which she spent exclusively with the second grade, I observed 11 instances of Quechua utterances.[2] Clearly, if one considers how many utterances may occur in the space of one minute (on the average, 5 to 15), these do not amount to even one percent use of Quechua in the classroom.

I describe type of Quechua use in terms of five categories of teacher talk and types of switch. The categories of teacher talk are the five shown in Table 1, drastically reduced from 22 acts defined by Sinclair & Coulthard (1975: 40–44).[3] Types of switch are the three shown in Table 2: Quechua alone, Quechua translation, and code-switching.

Profesor Gregorio's use of Quechua was, in all four cases, a direct translation of a preceding word or sentence in Spanish. He used Quechua to direct a student who failed to respond when directed in Spanish: *Siéntate, siéntate, tiyariy* 'Sit down, sit down, sit down';[4] to elicit a response: *Mira ve, no es cierto, hinachu, manachu?* 'Look, isn't that so, isn't that so?'; and to reprimand a student's performance: *Es flojo, qilla* 'He's lazy, he's lazy'.

Table 2 presents a tabulation and some examples of all observed instances of Sra Sara's Quechua use over a six-month period in multiple lessons. Note that over half (57%) of all use of Quechua was in direct translation of a preceding use of Spanish. Second, use of Quechua occurred in all five categories of teacher talk, though very infrequently (5% of total

TABLE 1 *Five categories of teacher talk*

Information	(I):	provides information.
		Q'umir q'aytu kanqa sapankunapaq.
		'The green thread will be for the ones.'
Elicitation	(E):	requests a linguistic response.
		Imawan qallarin?
		'What does it start with?'
Direction	(D):	requests a non-linguistic response.
		Hawatan lluqsiychis chay mana atindiqkuna.
		'Those who are not paying attention please go outside.'
Metastatement	(M):	Helps pupils see structure of lesson ... helps them understand the purpose of the subsequent exchange (Sinclair & Coulthard, 1975: 43). Includes summaries, reviews.
		Kunan kaymanta qallarisunchis.
		'Now we'll begin from here.'
Evaluation	(V):	Includes praise, reprimand, and simple acknowledgement.
		Mana allinchu chayqa.
		'That's not right.'

utterances) in evaluative talk. Third, in directive and elicitative talk, Quechua translation was used more (75% and 82% of directive and elicitative Quechua utterances, respectively), while in metastatements, Quechua alone was used more (70%). Finally, the occurrence of intra-sentential code-switching was minimal (10% of total Quechua utterances).

TABLE 2 *Teacher Quechua use in non-bilingual second grade (by utterance)*

	TYPE OF SWITCH			
	Q alone[1]	Q translation[2]	Code-switching[3]	TOTAL
TYPE OF TALK				
Information	2	6	3	11
Elicitation	1	6	1	8
Direction	2	9	0	11
Metastatement	7	3	0	10
Evaluation	2	0	0	2
TOTAL	14	24	4	42

EXAMPLES

Direction statements using Quechua translation:
   Van a guardar sus bolsitas adentro, ukhuman waqaychay.
   'Put your bags away /Sp./, put them away /Q./.' (8–18–83).
   Tres, tres, tres, kinsa [directing them to write 3].
   'Three, three, three /Sp./, three /Q./' (8–18–83).

Information statements using Quechua translation, the first one followed by a direction statement in Quechua alone:
   Este cuatro está de cabeza, se ha caido, urmaykun, sayarichiy.
   'This four is upside down, it has fallen /Sp./, it has fallen, stand it up' /Q./. (8–18–83).
   Van a dibujar lo que el hombre ha hecho ... lo que el hombre no ha hecho, ... imachus kan runaq ruwasqan.
   'You are going to draw what man has made, ... what man has not made /Sp./ ... what man has made /Q./.' (8–19–83).

Elicitations using Quechua translation:
   Son lo mismo? Kikinchu? Kaqllachu?
   'Are they the same? /Sp./ Are they the same, the same? /Q./.' (8–26–83).
   Tenemos tres ovejitas, quiero matar ocho, ¿se puede? atikunchu?
   'We have three lambs, I want to kill eight, can it be done? /Sp./, can it be done /Q./?' (8–26–83).

TABLE 2 *Continued*

Metastatements using Quechua alone:
  Pichá mana urmachinqa kayllamanta.
  'Whoever doesn't knock it off here /Q./.' (9–23–83).
  Paqarin qankuna mana hamunkichischu. Nuqayku llaqtata risaqku,
  kunan ichaqa palabrata yachasun, ya?
  'Tomorrow you will not come. We'll be going to town. But for now,
  let's learn these words, ok? /Q./' (10–20–83).

---

1. *Q alone*: a complete statement of new content in Quechua. May or may not be followed by translation into Spanish, but Spanish never precedes.
2. *Q translation*: a direct and immediate translation of either a word or entire sentence preceding in Spanish.
3. *Code-switching*: use of Quechua within a Spanish utterance, that is not a direct translation of a preceding Spanish word or phrase.

Based on the detailed observations of these six non-PEEB teachers and more casual observation of other Puno teachers in approximately fifteen schools visited for one to two days each throughout the period of the two-year study, the amount and type of teacher Quechua use in non-bilingual classrooms can be characterized as follows:

1. Amount: Teachers in non-bilingual classrooms use Quechua less than 1% of lesson time. This is far less than the amount they believe they use, as indicated by their responses in interviews and in the School Language/Teacher Attitude Questionnaire administered to six teachers (see Hornberger, 1988: 134, 254–256).
2. Type of Talk: When teachers in non-bilingual classrooms do use Quechua, it may occur in any of the five teacher-talk categories, but is least usual in evaluative teacher-talk.
3. Type of Switches:
   a. When teachers do use Quechua in non-bilingual classrooms, it is most often in direct translation of a preceding use of Spanish, especially in elicitative or directive speech.
   b. When teachers in non-bilingual classrooms do use Quechua alone, it is most often in metastatements.
   c. The highest incidence of code-switching (for example, 3 out of the 4 code-switching utterances for Sra Sara) is in informative teacher talk. This is difficult to explain, but it may be due to the fact that practically all of the information content that teachers in non-bilingual classrooms convey is in Spanish. Accordingly, teachers may code-switch in order to make the content both topically and culturally more intelligible to students.

Teacher Quechua use in bilingual classrooms

In amount, teacher Quechua use in bilingual classrooms far exceeded that in non-bilingual classrooms, constituting, by conservative estimate, at least 1/3 to 1/2 of lesson time. An exact estimate was difficult to ascertain due to the variation in language distribution behaviors of the different teachers. Profesor Victor's patterns of language use, for example, varied from class to class and from day to day: some classes were taught virtually in Spanish and others virtually in Quechua, while on other days classes were taught more or less half in Quechua and half in Spanish. Nevertheless, overall, out of 710 minutes of lesson time observed over a period of six months, I estimate that Profesor Victor used Quechua at least 1/3 to 1/2 of the time in lesson content in his class. The proportion of Sr Sergio's use of Quechua with the third grade class was similar, as observed in 245 minutes of lesson time in one month. In the first grade classroom, however, Sr Sergio used Quechua well over half the time, as observed in 460 minutes of lesson time over a period of 5 months.

The second significant difference between teacher Quechua use in non-bilingual and bilingual classrooms relates to code-switching. Tables 3 and 4 present tabulations of teacher Quechua use in one lesson each for Sr Sergio (Table 3) and Profesor Victor (Table 4). Whereas teachers in

TABLE 3 *Teacher Quechua use in bilingual first grade[1] (by utterance)*

	TYPE OF SWITCH			
	Q alone	Q translation	Code-switching	TOTAL
TYPE OF TALK				
Information	10	0	1	11
Elicitation	66	0	0	66
Direction	11	0	2	13
Metastatement	3	0	1	4
Evaluation	79	0	0	79
TOTAL	169	0	4	173

1. Tables 3 and 4 are not comparable to Table 2 since 3 and 4 represent Quechua use in one lesson each, while 2 represents total instances of Quechua use over a 6 month period in multiple lessons.

TABLE 4 *Teacher Quechua use in bilingual second grade*[1] *(by utterance)*

	TYPE OF SWITCH			
	Q alone	Q translation	Code-switching	TOTAL
TYPE OF TALK				
Information	71	0	0	71
Elicitation	34	0	0	34
Direction	43	0	1	44
Metastatement	8	0	0	8
Evaluation	21	1	0	22
TOTAL	177	1	1	179

1. Tables 3 and 4 are not comparable to Table 2 since 3 and 4 represent Quechua use in one lesson each, while 2 represents total instances of Quechua use over a 6 month period in multiple lessons.

non-bilingual classrooms used Quechua most often in translating a preceding use of Spanish, teachers in bilingual classrooms, when they used Quechua, used it almost exclusively as a medium of instruction, neither translating a preceding utterance in Spanish, nor code-switching between Spanish and Quechua within sentences. Though their classroom language involved switching from Quechua to Spanish and back again, the switching occurred between utterances.

There were marked differences as to the distribution of teacher-talk associated with the use of Quechua. In particular, the categories of evaluative, elicitative, and informative talk are salient in teacher Quechua use in bilingual classrooms. Note that elicitation and evaluation are particularly strong categories of Quechua teacher talk for Sr Sergio (Table 3), and information and direction are strong categories for Profesor Victor (Table 4). The use of particular categories themselves may reflect the effects of the particular lesson or teaching styles within each case: Sr Sergio was giving his pupils practice in reading aloud, and Profesor Victor was instructing his pupils to carry out a particular activity simultaneously with him.

Nevertheless, the use of *Quechua* in these categories is a direct consequence of the bilingual program. In both bilingual classrooms, and in contrast to the non-bilingual classrooms, the information content being conveyed was in Quechua. In the lessons represented by these tables, Sr

Sergio was teaching his class some of the first words in their Quechua reader *Kusi*, and Profesor Victor was teaching his class the use of the PEEB mathematical device termed *yupana*. It was this context which supported the use of Quechua consistently in all categories of teacher talk and which also produced a high degree of interaction with pupils. Such interaction was in marked contrast to the reticence and minimal response typical of Quechua-speaking children in the non-bilingual classrooms. In Profesor Victor's class, the pupils were actively carrying out the directions conveyed by the teacher. In Sr Sergio's class, the pupils were actively giving linguistic responses to the teacher's elicitations, which in turn produced the teacher's evaluations.

Moreover, there were other differences in teacher talk in Quechua in the bilingual classrooms that do not show up on the Tables. Whereas in the non-bilingual classrooms the teacher's Quechua utterances were often only short, truncated segments in the midst of lengthy Spanish utterances, in the bilingual classrooms the Quechua utterances were generally complete and well-formed utterances. Since Quechua is a language particularly rich in markers tying discourse to previous and following sentences,[5] this difference is significant. Compare, for example, the following uses of Quechua in the non-bilingual and bilingual classrooms.

From a non-bilingual classroom (with use of Quechua underlined):

Tenemos tres ovejitas, quiero matar ocho, ¿se puede? Atikunchu? 'We have three sheep, I want to kill eight, is it possible? Is it possible?'

From a bilingual classroom (9–15–82)[6] (in Quechua only, with Quechua discourse-tying markers underlined);

Kunan nuqa churasaq ahinata, qankunapis churallankichistaq. 'Now I'll put this like this, and you do it too.'

Huksitutallawan yapaykusunman. 'Now we'll just put one more again.'

Furthermore, grammatical morphemes serve to tie discourse together, as in the examples below, where the *-yuq* ('possessor of') nominal suffix and the *-n* (3rd person singular) verbal inflection both refer back to the previously mentioned subject, *usa* 'lice.'

Chakiyuqchu manachu? 'Do they have feet or not?'

Imata mikhun? 'What do they eat?'

More is involved here than the difference between single words and complete sentences. Teacher Quechua use in the bilingual classrooms reflects the nuances of grammatical structure which are an integral part of the language. These are features of Quechua discourse which were largely missing in teacher Quechua use in non-bilingual classrooms, but which, of course, help to contribute to full language development in pupils.

Cummins (1982) has distinguished between context-embedded and context-reduced language proficiency, where the former refers to the ability to grasp the content of a linguistic message when it is embedded in a 'flow of meaningful context', and the latter refers to the ability to grasp the content of a linguistic message when that context is very much reduced. Given that the classroom is widely recognized as a relatively context-reduced environment, the significance of teacher talk which provides as much 'context embedding' as possible seems clear.

In summary, teacher Quechua use in bilingual classrooms is both quantitatively and qualitatively different from teacher Quechua use in non-bilingual classrooms: teachers in the bilingual classrooms use significantly more Quechua, a more linguistically complete Quechua, more Quechua for primary communication (Quechua alone), and more Quechua for information content (informative, elicitative, evaluative talk).

In the bilingual classroom, then, the use of Quechua is expanded—absolutely, linguistically, and sociolinguistically. When we consider this in the light of Jacobson's argument about bilingual methodology, we conclude that the PEEB's bilingual methodology is one including maintenance and development of the Quechua language. When we consider it in the light of what we know about language learning, we cannot help but conclude that Quechua children will achieve higher levels of language proficiency in their L1, Quechua, in the bilingual classroom than they did in the non-bilingual classroom. I am arguing that this fact, too, must be counted among the criteria for evaluating the success of the Puno bilingual education program. Indeed, I am arguing that children's language proficiency in the L1 must be counted among the criteria for evaluating the success of any bilingual education program.

Acknowledgements

The research on which this paper is based was carried out in 1982 and 1983 with the permission and support of the Proyecto Experimental de Educación Bilingüe-Puno (Convenio Perú-República Federal de Alemania) in Puno, Peru, the Dirección Departamental de Educación in Puno, Peru, and the Instituto Nacional de Investigación y Desarrollo de la Educación

(INIDE) in Lima, Peru. Financial support came from the Inter-American Foundation and the U.S. Department of Education (Fulbright-Hays). Their assistance is gratefully acknowledged.

An earlier version of this paper was presented at a Colloquium on Language Planning and Teaching in Multilingual Countries at the 1987 TESOL Convention, Miami, Florida, April. I am grateful for comments by those who attended the Symposium.

Notes to Chapter 9

1. Following local custom, I refer to the directors of the schools as Sr and Sra, to the teachers as Profesor or Profesora, and to the _Wawa Wasi_ promoters as Srta.
2. Lest these seem insignificant quantities of time, it should be kept in mind that, for example, the 860 minutes of time-on-task represent only a fraction of time spent in school. Time-on-task represents only 15% of time spent in class, and class-time represents approximately 40% of time spent in school. Therefore, these 860 minutes of time-on-task were garnered from approximately 238 hours of observed schooltime. Similarly all other citations of time-on-task in the chapter represent approximately the following amounts of schooltime:

	Time-on-task	_Observed schooltime_
Prof. Gregorio	860 minutes	238 hours
Sra Sara 1–2	1175 minutes	327 hours
Sra Sara 2	675 minutes	188 hours
Prof. Victor	710 minutes	197 hours
Sr Sergio 3	245 minutes	68 hours
Sr Sergio 1	460 minutes	128 hours

3. Of Sinclair and Coulthard's 22 acts, four (bid, acknowledge, reply and react) refer to pupil, rather than teacher, acts; two (aside and silent stress) are not included here as they are considered irrelevant to my present purpose; two (marker and cue) are not included since their occurrence in Quechua was extremely rare; and nine are incorporated into the five categories. Specifically, elicitation and direction incorporate starter, prompt, clue, check, nomination and loop; evaluation incorporates accept; and metastatement incorporates comment and conclusion.
   I take the liberty of reducing the catalog of acts in this way since my purposes in analyzing teacher talk are different from Sinclair and Coulthard's. I am interested only in broadly outlining the types of teacher talk which occur in Quechua within lesson time. Sinclair and Coulthard, on the other hand, were interested in analyzing the flow of discourse in the classroom, and in understanding how the various acts form moves which in turn constitute the boundaries and teaching exchanges that make up a lesson. Such an analysis of the discourse in the

Visallani and Kinsachata classrooms would also be of significant value, but would be beyond the scope of the present study.
4. Underlining indicates that a different language is being used.
5. These discourse-tying markers are usually enclitic particles which serve a trans-sentential function in Quechua pragmatics.

Examples are: -*taq* 'and'; -*pis* 'also'; -*lla* -*taq* 'and also'; -*wan* 'in addition'; -*llawan* 'and also in addition'; -*ña* 'now, already'; -*ñataq* 'and now'; -*raq* 'still'; -*qa*, marking primary topic; -*mi*, marking secondary topic. They may also be unbound morphemes, such as: *hinaqa* 'so, then'.
6. A date within parentheses refers to an observation or quote in my field journal on that date.

References

CUMMINS, J. 1982, Tests, achievement, and bilingual students. *Focus* 9, 1–7.

HORNBERGER, N.H. 1988, *Bilingual Education and Language Maintenance: A Southern Peruvian Quechua Case*. Dordrecht: Foris.

JACOBSON, R. 1987, Allocating two languages as a key feature of a bilingual methodology. Paper presented at the 16th Annual International Bilingual/Bicultural Education Conference, Denver, CO.

SINCLAIR, J.M. and COULTHARD, M. 1975, *Towards an Analysis of Discourse: The English used by Teachers and Pupils*. London: Oxford University Press.

SPINDLER, G. 1982, *Doing the Ethnography of Schooling: Educational Anthropology in Action*. New York: Holt, Rinehart and Winston.

10 Code-switching in beginning foreign language teaching

GERALD S. GIAUQUE and CHRISTOPHER M. ELY

Jacobson (e.g. 1983) has proposed and tested a model which incorporates the use of code-switching (CS) in the teaching of content courses in bilingual programs. In this chapter, we suggest that CS can be used to advantage not only in bilingual content-based instruction, as Jacobson's results suggest, but in foreign language teaching as well. We begin with a brief rationale for the CS procedure, followed by a description of some of the more important aspects of the procedure. Finally, we summarize the preliminary research findings of a modest study of the use of CS in teaching university French. This discussion will, we hope, indicate that CS can be an effective vehicle for the teaching of foreign languages at the beginning level.

Rationale and underlying principles

What is the purpose of using code-switching in the foreign language (FL) classroom? The chief goal is to enable teachers to conduct their class largely in the target language even at the early stages of the language learning process. CS addresses a problem inherent in foreign language classes: the tension between the desire of the teacher to use the target language exclusively and the need of the student to understand as much as possible of what is being taught (see Giauque, 1985). In addition, the intent of the CS procedure is to motivate beginning students to use as much of the FL as they can for real-life communication.

The basic principle of using CS in teaching foreign languages is that the teacher speaks the foreign language using many cognate words, and uses CS (i.e. code-switches into English) to communicate those words which are not cognates in the target language. As a result, students learn that it is possible to understand a great deal of the target language at a very early stage in their learning experience. From the outset, they are taught, indirectly, to listen for cognate words; the teacher's use of English words when cognates do not exist in the target language provides additional contextual clues for understanding. We thus have the best of both worlds: students comprehend a large amount, while at the same time, the teacher uses English only quite sparingly.

The central difference between this type of CS in teaching and that proposed by Jacobson (1983: 2) for bilingual elementary classrooms is that the code-switching occurs not inter-sententially, but intra-sententially, as it does in adolescent and adult CS outside the classroom (see e.g. Attinasi *et al.*, 1982; Coballes-Vega, 1980; Faltis, 1984; Gumperz & Hernandez-Chavez, 1972; Koike, 1987).

In teaching foreign languages in the United States, we must recognize that English speakers are very fortunate that the commonly-taught languages (French, German, and Spanish) are related to English; this relationship should be exploited to a much greater degree than is traditionally the case. In particular, the study of vocabulary, and most importantly, that of cognate words, needs to be brought into the mainstream of foreign language teaching in this country. It is likely that if students of foreign languages knew that the study of cognate words could help them understand a comparatively large amount of FL material, they would be more highly motivated to study languages.

The CS procedure

During the first week of CS, students are introduced to the notion of cognates and their importance in learning a foreign language. Pronunciation is also discussed here, since it has been found that students need to learn and be given practice with some of the more important sound–symbol correlations if they are to be successful in listening to cognates and using them in speech. After students have learned of the existence and potential of cognates and learned how to pronounce them, they are encouraged to listen for cognates in the teacher's speech.

In recent years, great emphasis has been placed on the notion that comprehension should precede oral production in the study of a foreign language (see e.g. Nagle & Sanders, 1986; Postovsky, 1982; Sheerin, 1987; Winitz, 1981). In CS, the teacher always seeks oral feedback from the students, even during the first weeks of the course. However, in consonance with the 'comprehension-first' position, the responses of the students are expected to be short, and in almost all cases, they consist of just one word, 'yes', or 'no', in response to such questions as: 'Do you understand?' 'Do you have a question?' 'Do you want me to say that again?' (questions which are spoken in either the FL or a code-switched version of the FL). By requiring and obtaining such feedback, the teacher learns if the students have understood what she has said (and thus she can repeat and clarify words, expressions, and concepts where necessary). In addition, by being allowed to respond to natural and meaningful questions, even in the form of short responses, the students become accustomed to the idea that they are learning the foreign language for real communication, not just as an academic exercise.

The teacher's use of CS makes it relatively easy for the students themselves to begin using CS from the earliest stages. By speaking it herself, the teacher provides a model of how CS works, which implicitly encourages the students to engage in CS themselves. Moreover, in addition to modeling CS, it is necessary for the teacher to explain overtly the reason for using CS. She can say, for instance, that students typically assume that FL teachers expect them to speak only English or only the target language. However, since beginning language students have almost no facility in the target language, they simply never try to use it. In the CS procedure, however, the students learn a little language at a time as they try to use the target language starting from the first day. Since total use of the FL is out of the question for beginning students, the only way to achieve actual and 'full' communication in class is by code-switching.

Since the basic grammatical structure of the student's native tongue is utilized for a brief period, words of the target language may be 'plugged in' in a manner that may surprise a native speaker of that language. However, CS is used for only a comparatively short period of time; by the third or fourth week of the semester, the teacher is conducting most of the class exclusively in the target language. She will still use many cognates, but the grammar structures of her speech will basically be those of the target language. Thus, CS is not a 'method' to be used throughout the entire year, but is a procedure leading to the stage where the class is conducted entirely in the target language.

The teacher is especially careful to use CS when students initiate conversations with her (before, during, and after class) about such subjects as the course material, testing procedures, and personal concerns not directly related to the course, such as excuses, make-up work, etc. If students try to use nothing but English, the teacher, rather than allowing them to do so, encourages them (again and again, if necessary) to use CS (not the target language, which, of course, the students are unable to do). If on one occasion a student continues to resist the use of CS, the teacher relents, but she makes it clear that she will expect more use of the target language (in code-switched form) in future discussions with her.

If students want to use CS in a one-to-one discussion with the teacher, but simply cannot find the necessary words, the teacher encourages them to write their sentence or question on a piece of paper. Rather than responding immediately to that utterance, she draws students' attention to the cognate words of the sentence, or helps them find cognate words, and has them pronounce those cognate words as words in the target language. For example, let us imagine that the student wants to say 'When will the test be?' The student may not even try to say it in the FL, but speaks in the native language. The teacher may then feign non-comprehension, saying 'What?' in the FL. The student may of course exhibit an air of disgust, but the teacher hands him a pencil and scrap of paper (always kept nearby for such occasions) and says, in the FL, 'Write!' The student writes his question in English, and the teacher then crosses out or erases the student's words 'will' and 'be' and writes 'is'. The sentence now reads (in English) 'When is the test?' (This change in tenses is necessary at the early stages, since the word for 'will' has not yet been introduced.) If the class is beyond the second week of the semester, the student already knows three of these words, 'when', 'is', and 'the'. The teacher crosses out words like these which the student should know and either writes in the FL equivalents or, in the target language, asks the student to write them himself. The teacher then tells the student (in the FL), 'Read that'. Only after the student has read the sentence does the teacher answer the question.

What has the teacher done? She has responded to the student, although she has probably taken longer to do so than he wished. But more importantly, she has made an attempt to teach him that (1) the FL is for real communication, not just for exercises; (2) by thinking about what they have previously learned, students can indeed construct meaningful utterances in the FL.

The teacher code-switches, not only while speaking, but also while writing. She will write an expression on the chalkboard in English, and pronounce the expression (or most of it) in the target language. Alternatively, she will write an expression of two or more words on the board in code-switched form. In doing so, she teaches the students how to spell certain expressions in the target language. In addition, she implicitly teaches the students that CS can be written, and this helps solidify in their minds the idea that CS is systematic and consistent, not random or disorganized. Thus, writing CS, as well as speaking it, helps to overcome negative attitudes toward CS that some students may hold.

In the CS procedure, the teacher is not alone in writing code-switched sentences in the foreign language. The students themselves are also taught to do so. It is true, of course, that the main purpose of most foreign language courses is to help the students learn to speak the foreign language. But reading and writing are also important skills, both intrinsically and in support of speaking. One way in which CS can be used in teaching is through the use of a workbook. For example, as part of the unit on cognates and sound–symbol correlations described above, the students can use a workbook containing study questions keyed to explanatory material in the text. The students are told to answer these questions not in English but in 'Franglais'.[1] The following is a brief excerpt from the workbook that has been developed by the first author:

> Answer these study questions according to the instructions given by the teacher in class. Write in franglais, unless you are specifically told not to by your teacher! Complete sentences are not necessary, but franglais IS necessary. 'But what is franglais?' you ask. Answer: It is half français (French) and half anglais (English). Merge them together and you get ... FRAN-GLAIS. In order to write franglais, you substitute a FRENCH word whenever you can for an English word. 'But I don't KNOW any French words', you may say. 'That's the reason I'm taking this class!' Answer: Yes, you do. Most words ending in -tion in English are French words. And you know quite a few such words. Most words that end in -ty in English end in -té in French. You might not know any French words today, but by TOMORROW, you WILL know some, and as soon as you DO know some French words, I want you to use THEM instead of the English words. *UNDERLINE* any and all words you use which you THINK might be French words. By the time you finish these exercises in two weeks, you will already have a pretty respectable vocabulary, IF you follow these instructions.

> The following are examples of franglais: '*Je* do not comprehend what *franglais* is'. 'Your *explication* is *difficile* to *comprendre*'. '*Je* am having *difficulté* with this learning *activité*. The *information* is *insuffisante*'.

When the homework comes in, some is written entirely in English, despite the instructions to the contrary; a number of students, however, have ventured to use CS words. As the teacher scans the students' papers, she crosses out every occurrence of the word 'French' in their writing and replaces it with the word 'Français'. Likewise, the teacher underlines every English word which may be a French cognate (and can draw a smile above it). On every paper, particularly those containing no French at all, she writes 'Remember to write en franglais'. This is reiterated in class for several days regarding the following day's assignment, and after a few class periods, the students realize that the teacher is very serious about the use of 'Frenglish'. Soon, definite and indefinite articles begin to appear, not in English, but in French. Pronoun subjects also begin to appear as French words, as do some cognate words and certain conjugations of the verb 'to be'. Dates at the top of the paper, after having been corrected three days in a row, begin to take on the French form. From 5% (i.e. one French word for approximately two lines of English text) the amount of French increases to 10%, then 20%, and soon it is 33% to 50%.

Each day the teacher senses a growing sophistication in the use of the language as she seeks confirmation that the students understand. She calls the students' attention to the fact that 'a miracle' is occurring: it is becoming possible to conduct the class more and more in the target language, making less and less use of spoken English. (The teacher does, however, often continue to write on the chalkboard in English.) Within two weeks, teacher talk is at least 50% French.

It is, of course, necessary for the teacher to monitor her speech a great deal in order to use many cognate words and provide a great deal of context. However, if the teacher is sufficiently motivated to use this procedure, she will find that, with practice, she is able to think simultaneously in the two languages with little difficulty. A caution is in order here, however. The successes that Jacobson (1983) reports for the use of CS in the classroom apparently depend upon the fact that the teachers do not code-switch randomly, but use a carefully controlled procedure. Similarly, a teacher using CS and cognate words in foreign language teaching should also receive training or train herself to avoid random code-switching, which is of most dubious value.

An important issue to mention here is that of student resistance to the CS procedure. Such attitudes as the following sometimes surface: (1) 'It's too childish to speak in Frenglish, to say "je" every time I want to say "I"—I feel silly and embarrassed'; (2) 'It's too hard to slow down my speech and think about every word to see if I can say it in French—I feel stupid when I do it'; or (3) 'I've never heard of such a method— I'm not sure it will produce any results whatsoever'. Experience has shown that attempting to argue against these attitudes may be time-consuming and counter-productive. Instead, by simply showing her enthusiasm for CS, the teacher can greatly diminish negative attitudes. After the students have worked with CS for a period, they are much more likely to accept it and recognize its worth.

Research

Having briefly introduced the philosophy and methodology of teaching foreign languages with CS, let us describe now the first research conducted to determine the results of using the procedure. It was decided that this exploratory study would concern itself with the attitudes of students toward the procedure.

The course in which the research was done was first-year, first-semester French (French 101). There were 30 students at the beginning of the semester, and 27 at the end (the three students who left the course were interviewed by graduate assistants).[2] The class met four days a week. Although the class was intended for students who had never before studied French, it was obvious from the first day of class that about 15 of them were 'faux débutants', that is, that they had had previous exposure to French. (No intentional changes in the procedure were made for these students; future research will be necessary to determine if students' prior FL experience influences attitudes towards CS.)

The research questionnaire was written by the first author and administered by a graduate student. The class was told that the instructor would not see the questionnaires which the students had filled out. These questionnaires were distributed to the students nine times during the 15-week semester: on the first day of class, on the second day of the class, and at the last class meeting of weeks 1, 2, 4, 6, 8, 11, and 15. All questionnaires (except the first two) were identical. (The first two questionnaires contained slightly different questions from the subsequent seven questionnaires.) If students were absent, the questionnaire was administered to them upon their return to class.

There were 10 research hypotheses investigated (the 'Q' numbers in parenthesis indicate the number of the questionnaire item corresponding to the hypothesis):

1. Few, if any, students have prior knowledge of what CS is; after several weeks, they evidence understanding of the concept (Q1).
2. Most students at first consider CS irrelevant to FL instruction; as

the semester progresses, they begin to think of CS in more positive terms (Q2).

3. Few, if any, students report using CS at the beginning of the semester; students report gradually increasing their use of CS during the semester (Q3).

4. Most students feel at the beginning of the course that the use of CS results in 'picking up bad habits'; this opinion largely disappears during the semester (Q4).

5. Few, if any, students have ever seen or heard of CS being used before (Q5—(this question was dropped after the first two surveys).

6. Students' opinions of the teacher's use of CS move from negative to positive during the semester (the following specific attitudes were surveyed—Q7a: disgust; Q7b: tension; Q7c: amusement; Q7d: curiosity; Q7e: confusion; Q7f: delight; Q7g: surprise; Q7h: interest; Q7i: some positive feelings; Q7j: some negative feelings; Q7k: feelings of frustration; Q7l: feelings of relief and freedom; Q7m: I really did not know what to think).

7. Students' attitudes toward CS as being 'comical' diminish during the semester (Q8).

8. During the semester, students increasingly feel that the use of CS is helpful in learning the foreign language (Q9).

9. At the beginning of the semester, the majority of students do not use CS outside the classroom; as the semester progresses, more and more students do so (Q10).

Results

Table 1 presents the results for the questionnaires. The table displays the nine administrations of the questionnaire (T1...T9), and the responses to the questions asked (Q1...Q9). Q6 is not represented in the table, since it was not a multiple response item (asking for further information about responses to Q3, Q4, or Q5).

The figures represent a weighted total of all answers for each question. If a student answered 'Not at all' on the survey form, that answer received a score of 1 point. The other possible responses and weightings were: 'Somewhat' (3 points); 'Yes, very much' (5 points); intermediate between 'Not at all' and 'Somewhat' (2 points); and intermediate between 'Somewhat' and 'Yes, very much' (4 points). Thus, on the first day, when 30 students responded to all the questions, the lowest possible number was 30 (30×1).

TABLE 1

	T1	T2	T3	T4	T5	T6	T7	T8	T9
Q1	31	36	43	86	108	122	128	128	129
Q2	6	8	69	80	99	109	119	127	130
Q3	1	2	47	60	71	78	84	85	89
Q4	14	12	96	86	80	75	65	67	60
Q5	30	31	30	34	39	45	46	54	61
Q7a	7	6	5	3	2	1	1	2	1
Q7b	14	12	11	10	9	6	4	4	3
Q7c	25	24	20	17	16	14	13	10	6
Q7d	10	10	9	9	7	7	4	3	3
Q7e	10	8	5	4	4	3	2	2	0
Q7f	7	8	9	11	12	14	14	17	18
Q7g	8	7	7	6	6	5	5	5	3
Q7h	11	10	10	9	8	6	5	5	4
Q7i	10	10	11	11	11	12	12	12	12
Q7j	20	19	18	15	10	9	8	8	6
Q7k	15	14	15	14	14	13	12	10	8
Q7l	4	4	6	6	7	6	6	6	6
Q7m	18	19	19	20	19	15	11	10	8
Q8	134	135	123	120	105	103	93	80	81
Q9	32	57	77	82	90	105	111	121	126
Q10	14	20	27	36	42	56	60	63	69

The response 'Yes, very much' was never given by all students completing the questionnaire; therefore, the highest possible total never occurred for any item. After T3, the highest possible total per item was 145, because one student had dropped; after T4, that number was 140; after T7, it was 135.

The T1 and T2 questionnaires instructed the students to skip questions 2, 3, and 4 if they had ever heard of or seen CS. On the first day of class, only three of the students indicated such previous contact with the procedure. The total number of points for those questions on the T1 and T2 surveys was therefore 15 (3 × 5).

At the end of the semester, the results of each questionnaire were plotted on a graph. Due to lack of space, that graph is omitted here, but it should be noted that in most cases, once a trend was established, that trend continued in the same direction during the semester. The only exceptions were: Q5 (at T3), Q7a (at T8), Q7k (at T3), Q7l (at T6), Q7m (at T5).

Discussion of results

The results were generally as expected. The hypotheses about students' perceptions of CS were supported by the data for attitudes throughout the semester. It should be noted, however, that the results for hypotheses 9 and 10 were somewhat modest. In general, though, it appears that, with exposure to CS, students accept the procedure and use it themselves. The last question in the survey is, of course, the most important one, and the results suggest that students feel CS can be helpful in teaching and learning a foreign language. Further research is currently contemplated that would compare the language achievement of students taught by means of CS with students instructed with more traditional procedures.

Concluding remarks

It is hoped that this chapter will encourage foreign language teaching professionals to make an unbiased examination of the usefulness of the CS procedure. In theory, at least, a natural area for growth in the use of CS would be in the teaching of Spanish as a foreign language, since the teachers of this language are often already more acquainted with the phenomenon of CS than are, say, teachers of French or German. Some of those teachers who are acquainted with the usefulness of CS in the instruction of Spanish-speaking bilinguals may well be relatively receptive to trying CS with their own pupils. However, up to the present there would seem to be among many teachers of Spanish (as a foreign language) a negative attitude toward code-switching (as manifested by Hispanic-Americans); these attitudes will need to be altered, perhaps by demonstrating the efficacy of the CS procedure. At present, it may be the teachers of French or German (and, in particular, native speakers of English, who may have fewer emotional ties to the FL) that are best suited to lead the way toward the increased use of CS in the foreign language classroom.

Notes to Chapter 10

1. It is true that terms such as 'Frenglish/franglais' and 'Spanglish/espanglish' have negative connotations for some professionals. However, these terms generally

e not a negative connotation, but merely a humorous one, to post-elementary students, most of whom have never heard them before. They have proved to be an effective way of fixing the concept in the students' minds.
2. One student dropped the class because he said he had decided he did not want to study a foreign language at that time. In addition, he had gotten a job and thought that he would not have enough time to study. He said his decision to drop was not at all related to the way the class was being conducted. A second student who dropped the class said that she did not like the teaching method employed—it 'confused' her. She had never before studied a foreign language, but found that her expectations differed from the classroom experience. She considered herself an average student. The third student dropped the class because she had been ill for nearly five weeks of the semester. She did not feel that she could do what was necessary to catch up.

References

ATTINASI, J., PEDRAZA, P., POPLACK, S. and POUSADA, A. 1982, Intergenerational perspectives on bilingualism: from community to classroom. (Final Report, ERIC Document Reproduction Service No. ED 232 435). New York: City University of New York, Centro de Estudios Puertorriqueños.

COBALLES-VEGA, C. 1980, A comparison of the form and function of code-switching of Chicano and Puerto Rican children. Doctoral Dissertation, University of Illinois at Urbana-Champaign, 1980. (*Dissertation Abstracts International* 41, 528–A).

FALTIS, C.J. 1984, Reading and writing in Spanish for bilingual college students: What's taught at school and what's used in the community. *Bilingual Review* 11, 21–32.

GIAUQUE, G.S. 1985, The first days of class. (ERIC Document Reproduction Service No. ED 264 739).

GUMPERZ, J.J. and HERNÁNDEZ-CHÁVEZ, E. 1972, Bilingualism, bidialectalism, and classroom interaction. In C.B. CAZDEN, V.P. JOHN and D. HYMES (eds), *Functions of Language in the Classroom*. New York: Teacher's College, Columbia University.

JACOBSON, R. 1983, Intersentential codeswitching: An educationally justifiable strategy. (ERIC Document Reproduction Service No. ED 231 221).

KOIKE, D.A. 1987, Code switching in the bilingual Chicano narrative. *Hispania* 70, 148–54.

NAGLE, S.J. and SANDERS, S.L. 1986, Comprehension theory and second language pedagogy. *TESOL Quarterly* 20, 9–26.

POSTOVSKY, V.A. 1982, Delayed oral practice. In R.W. BLAIR (ed.), *Innovative Approaches to Language Teaching* (pp. 67–76). Rowley, MA: Newbury House.

SHEERIN, S. 1987, Listening comprehension: Teaching or testing? *ELT Journal* 41, 126–31.

WINITZ, H. (ed.), 1981, *The Comprehension Approach to Foreign Language Instruction*. Rowley, MA: Newbury House.

About the contributors

Robert A. DeVillar (PhD Stanford University) is Assistant Professor of Bilingual and Computer Education at San Diego State University, Imperial Valley Campus. Before going to San Diego State, Professor DeVillar taught courses in bilingual teaching strategies at Sonoma State University and spent seven years in the computer industry, primarily in international management. He has traveled extensively, and has lived and studied in Spain and Mexico. In 1987, as a Teaching Fellow, Professor DeVillar developed and taught a course at the Stanford School of Education entitled 'Microcomputers in Instruction and Educational Equity'. His research interests are in the areas of computers, issues of educational equity, and bilingualism. He has published several articles on these topics.

Christopher M. Ely (PhD Stanford University) currently directs the English Language Institute at Ball State University in Muncie, Indiana, where he is also an Assistant Professor specializing in Second Language Education in the Department of English. His primary area of interest is language learning motivation. He has published on this and related topics in *Language Learning, The Modern Language Journal,* and *Foreign Language Annals.* Professor Ely was the recipient of the 1985 Birkmaier Award for Doctoral Dissertation Research, awarded by the American Council on the Teaching of Foreign Languages.

Christian J. Faltis (PhD Stanford University) is Associate Professor of Second Language and Bilingual Education at the University of Nevada-Reno, where he teaches courses in bilingual education, socio-cultural issues in education, teaching English as a second language, and curriculum development for language minority programs. Professor Faltis has worked with teachers at the University of Alabama, and outside of the United States in Tegucigalpa, where he held a Fulbright Professorship at the University of Honduras. He has also taught in Ecuador, Colombia, and the Dominican Republic. He has worked in a number of bilingual programs in California and was a teacher educator at the University of California, Davis. His

rch interests include effective bilingual instruction, teaching Spanish to
..ve speakers, and interaction in linguistically heterogeneous classrooms.
He has published in all three areas of interest.

Eugene E. Garcia (PhD University of Kansas) is Professor and Chair of
the Board of Studies in Education at the University of California, Santa
Cruz. An internationally known scholar, Professor Garcia has also held
teaching positions at Arizona State University and the University of
California, Santa Barbara. He completed a Post-Doctoral Fellowship in
Psycholinguistics at Harvard University. He has published a number of
significant books on bilingualism and bilingual education research. Among
his more well-known works are *Early Childhood Bilingualism*; *The
Mexican American Child*: *Language, Cognition, and Social Development*;
Advances in Bilingual Education Research (with Raymond Padilla); and
Language and Literacy Research in Bilingual Education (with Barbara
Flores). He is also widely published in language education journals.

Gerald S. Giauque (PhD University of Oregon) is Professor of Modern
Languages at Northern Arizona University, in Flagstaff, Arizona, where he
has taught French language and linguistics since 1976. Before going to
Northern Arizona, Professor Giauque was head of the Department of
Modern Languages at Georgia Institute of Technology. He participated in a
Fulbright Teacher Exchange to France in 1985–86, and has published a
number of pedagogically oriented articles in *Hispania*, *Modern Language
Journal*, and *Foreign Language Annals*. Over the last ten years, he has
developed a code-switching approach to teaching beginning level French to
college students.

Nancy H. Hornberger (PhD University of Wisconsin-Madison) graduated
cum laude from Harvard University with a major in Hispanic-American
History and Literature. She is presently an Assistant Professor in the
Language in Education Division of the Graduate School of Education,
University of Pennsylvania. Her dissertation on Quechua schooling in
southern Peru won first place in the 1987 National Association of Bilingual
Education Dissertations Competition. A book based upon her dissertation
research has recently appeared. Professor Hornberger has published her
research findings in a number of scholarly journals.

Rodolfo Jacobson (PhD University of Michigan) is Professor Emeritus in
Bilingual Education and Sociolinguistics at the University of Texas at San
Antonio. His involvement with language minority children spans nearly 40
years. Formally trained in linguistics, Professor Jacobson taught ESL at

Michigan for four years before moving on to the State University of New York at Cortland. He took a position at University of Texas at San Antonio in 1974, and has been there ever since. He recently completed a Fulbright Professorship at the University of Malaya, in Malaysia. Since 1959, he has published more than two dozen books and articles on language, language learning, and bilingual education. He developed the only bilingual teaching methodology native to the United States, the New Concurrent Approach, and has trained teachers to use it in a variety of educational settings. His most recent work is the soon to be published collection of papers entitled *Codeswitching as a Worldwide Phenomenon*.

Barbara J. Merino (PhD Stanford University) received her doctorate in Education and Linguistics from Stanford, holds an MA in Italian from UCLA, and a BA in French and History from the University of Southern California. She has taught Italian, Spanish, English and French to students ranging in age from pre-school to university. She is currently an Associate Professor in Education and Linguistics at the University of California, Davis, where she also coordinates the Bilingual and Foreign Language credentials program. Her principal research interests are in language acquisition and language loss in bilingual children, classroom processes, language assessment, and curriculum development. She has published her research on these topics in a variety of scholarly journals.

Robert D. Milk (PhD Stanford University) holds advanced degrees in Linguistics and Education from Stanford University. He has taught in secondary schools in the United States and in normal schools in Peru. Currently, he is an Associate Professor of Bicultural-Bilingual Studies at the University of Texas at San Antonio. He was awarded a Fulbright Fellowship as a Senior Lecturer in Peru, and has directed two Title VII Bilingual Teacher Training projects at UTSA. His articles have appeared in *TESOL Quarterly, NABE Journal, Journal of Multilingual and Multicultural Development, Bilingual Review*, and *Hispanic Journal of Behavioral Sciences*.

Raymond V. Padilla (PhD University of California, Berkeley) is currently the Director of the Hispanic Research Center at Arizona State University, where he is also Professor of Education. Before going to Arizona State, Professor Padilla taught at Eastern Michigan University in Ypsilanti. Professor Padilla served as editor of 3 volumes on *Ethnoperspectives in Bilingual Education* (1979–1982). Vol. 1 was entitled: *Bilingual Education and Public Policy in the United States*. Vol. 2 was on *Theory in Bilingual Education*. Vol. 3 focused on *Bilingual Education Technology*. More

\tly, he edited with Eugene Garcia a volume on *Advances in Bilingual ..ation Research*.

J. David Ramirez (PhD Stanford University) completed his doctorate in 1981 in Psychological Studies, with an emphasis in Early Childhood Education. Dr. Ramirez is currently Senior Research Associate for Aguirre International in San Mateo, California. His research interests are primarily in the areas of bilingual education program evaluation, and the effectiveness of immersion education programs for language minority children. He has conducted nation-wide research projects in transitional bilingual education programs, and has evaluated student exchange programs in Central America.

Judith Walker de Felix (PhD University of Florida) is currently an Associate Professor of Second Language Education at the University of Houston, in Texas. A former public school teacher in Texas and Kansas, Professor Walker de Felix has also taught at Dominican College. She is the author of *Education in Two Languages*, and has published a number of articles in bilingual education and second language journals. One of her major interests is preparing effective bilingual and English as a second language teachers using a strong research base. She is currently directing a Title VII Bilingual Teaching Training project based on effective bilingual teaching strategies research.

Index

Note: Numbers in italics refer to tables and figures.